ANALOG ANCHORS

ANALOG ANCHORS

GROUNDING YOURSELF IN THE DIGITAL TIDE

David Olubiyi

Dabim Support Services Inc.

To the seekers of balance in a world that spins ever faster,

To those who find beauty in the simplicity of a handwritten note, the warmth of a face-to-face conversation, and the tranquility of unplugged moments,

To my family, whose unwavering support and love remind me every day of what truly matters in this digital age,

And to the future generations, who will navigate the digital tides with the anchors we leave behind,
May this book serve as a compass, guiding you towards a harmonious and mindful coexistence with technology.

With all my heart,

David Olubiyi

Contents

Foreword

In a world where our lives are increasingly intertwined with digital devices, where the boundary between the virtual and the real blurs, David Olubiyi's "Analog Anchors: Grounding Yourself in the Digital Tide" emerges as a timely and essential guide.

We are sailing in uncharted digital waters. As we navigate these vast and often overwhelming seas, David Olubiyi acts as our lighthouse, illuminating the path to a balanced life. His unique perspective, rooted in a deep understanding of physics and a passionate commitment to mindfulness, provides a fresh and much-needed approach to managing our digital existence.

"Analog Anchors" is not just a book; it is a journey. A journey that invites us to pause, reflect, and reconnect with the often-forgotten tactile and tangible aspects of life. David challenges us to question our digital habits, to recognize the power and the limitations of technology, and to embrace the beauty of the analog world that surrounds us.

Throughout these pages, you will find a blend of personal insights, scientific understanding, and practical advice. David's voice is one of empathy and wisdom, encouraging us to reclaim control over our digital lives. He does not advocate for a complete disconnection from the digital world; rather, he guides us towards a harmonious relationship with technology, one where our human needs and values take precedence.

As you embark on this enlightening read, prepare to engage with stories that resonate, strategies that empower, and a vision that inspires. "Analog Anchors: Grounding Yourself in the Digital Tide" is more than a book – it is a movement towards a more intentional, balanced, and fulfilling life in the digital age.

Welcome to a journey of rediscovery, where each page turns a new leaf towards understanding how we can anchor ourselves amidst the relentless waves of the digital tide.

Preface

As you hold this book in your hands, amidst a world pulsating with digital signals and screens, you embark on a journey that is both personal and universal. "Analog Anchors: Grounding Yourself in the Digital Tide" is born out of a deep desire to bridge the gap between our digital lives and our inherent need for tangible, real-world connections.

My journey into writing this book began as a quest for understanding – understanding how the laws of physics, which govern the universe, also subtly influence our interactions with technology. As a physicist, I have always been fascinated by the forces and principles that shape our existence. However, it was my personal experiences with the overwhelming tide of digital information and connectivity that led me to explore how these scientific concepts could be applied to our everyday lives.

This book is an amalgamation of my years of research, reflections, and interactions with people from various walks of life who shared their struggles and triumphs in balancing their digital and analog lives. Through these pages, I seek to offer not just insights but practical tools – the 'analog anchors' – that can help us stay grounded in a world that often feels adrift in digital currents.

"Analog Anchors" is more than just a guide to disconnecting from the digital world; it is a manifesto for rekindling our appreciation for the physical, the tangible, and the human. It is about finding joy in the rustle of pages, the warmth of a conversation, and the beauty of a sunset unfiltered through a lens.

I invite you to join me on this exploration of how we can embrace technology without letting it overpower our sense of presence, connection, and wonder in the real world. May the chapters that follow serve as a compass in your journey, guiding you to find your own anchors in this ever-changing digital tide.

Welcome aboard.

Letter to the Reader

Dear Reader,

As you turn the pages of "Analog Anchors: Grounding Yourself in the Digital Tide," I want to extend my heartfelt gratitude for joining me on this journey. This book is not just a collection of words and ideas; it is a conversation between us, a shared exploration of how we can live more fully in a world dominated by digital influences.

You and I are part of an unprecedented era. An era where the boundaries between the digital and the physical blur, where the pace of technological advancement often outstrips our ability to adapt. This book was born from a deep-seated concern for our collective well-being in this digital age and a hope that we can find harmony amidst the chaos.

My aim is not to admonish technology; after all, it has brought immeasurable advancements and conveniences. Instead, I seek to offer a perspective that helps us navigate the digital landscape with mindfulness and intention. Through "Analog Anchors," I hope to provide you with the tools and insights to create a more balanced life, one where technology serves you, not the other way around.

Each chapter of this book is designed to engage, challenge, and inspire you. You will find within these pages a blend of personal anecdotes, scientific explorations, and practical advice. I encourage you to read with an open mind and heart, to question and reflect, and most importantly, to apply these ideas in a way that resonates with your unique life.

Remember, this book is not an end but a beginning. It is the start of a conscious journey towards finding and maintaining your equilibrium in the digital tide. I hope that "Analog Anchors" becomes a companion in your quest for a more grounded, present, and fulfilling life.

Thank you for embarking on this journey with me. May we both discover new ways to thrive in this digital age.

With warm regards,

David Olubiyi

Prologue

The Unstoppable Digital Wave

The dawn of the 21st century heralded an era of technological marvels, propelling us into a sea of digital innovation with unrelenting force. This unstoppable digital wave has permeated every facet of human life, from the way we wake to the manner in which we rest our minds at night. Smart devices, apps, social media—each a droplet in the vast ocean of digital engagement—promised to bridge distances, to simplify complexities, and to amplify our human potential.

As the wave swelled, it carried us on a current of infinite possibility. The world shrank in the palm of our hands; information, once the province of libraries and institutions, became instantaneous and ubiquitous. Our voices, magnified by the reach of the internet, found audiences across the globe, and our capacity for innovation seemed boundless.

Yet, as we marveled at our newfound abilities to connect and create, a subtle undertow was at work. The same technologies that delivered freedom and efficiency also began to commandeer our time, chip away at our concentration, and subtly rewrite the script of our daily lives. The tools we created to serve us slowly started to steer us, and the wave we rode began to ride us.

The digital wave, unstoppable as it is, need not be a force that pulls us under. There is a way to coexist with this mighty tide—to draw from its strength without getting lost in its depths. This book is about finding equilibrium. It is about how we can plant our feet firmly in the soil of the physical world while we let our minds surf the digital expanse. It is about setting our Analog Anchors in the digital tide, and in doing so, reclaiming not just our time, but the very essence of what it means to live fully and authentically as human beings.

The Need for Anchoring

As we stand amidst this relentless digital surge, a quiet realization washes over us: the tools meant to be our servants subtly morphed into our masters. The same devices that promised liberation now often tether us with invisible chains of obligation and distraction. Our attention, divided and conquered by algorithms that know us all too well, leaves us adrift in a sea of digital noise, yearning for a compass to navigate these uncharted waters.

This is where the need for anchoring emerges—a primal call to secure ourselves to something foundational and unyielding in the face of constant change. Anchoring is not about rejecting the digital world; rather, it is about establishing a stronghold that keeps us from being swept away. It's about identifying and holding fast to the elements of life that remain constant and true in the physical world—our relationships, our health, our creativity, and our peace of mind.

Anchors are as unique as the individuals who cast them. For some, it may be the weight of a pen gliding across a journal page, for others, the rhythmic cadence of a morning run, or the quiet ritual of brewing a perfect cup of tea. These anchors ground us, reminding us of the world beyond our screens—a world rich with textures, flavors, sounds, and real-time, heartfelt interactions.

This book will guide you to discover and deploy your analog anchors—the practices and pursuits that can stabilize and enrich your life amidst the digital maelstrom. Through cultivating these anchors, we aim to build resilience against the pull of the digital tide, ensuring that we remain captains of our own ships, able to enjoy the digital world without becoming engulfed by it.

In the pages that follow, we embark on a journey to reclaim our autonomy in a world awash with pixels and notifications, where every beep and buzz beckons for our attention. "Analog Anchors: Grounding Yourself in the Digital Tide" is more than just a manual; it's a manifesto for a life lived with intention in the era of digital excess.

The digital tide surged quietly at first, becoming the backdrop of our daily lives. It promised endless connections and conveniences, and we welcomed it with open arms. But as its currents grew stronger, we found ourselves adrift, often more isolated in our hyper-connected world than we were before its arrival.

This book introduces the concept of 'Analog Anchors'—those tangible, sensory-rich activities and practices that tether us to the physical world. It is an invitation to find balance amidst the digital storm, to foster moments that require our presence, not just our screen time.

In the chapters to come, we will explore the neurological, psychological, and social ramifications of our digitally-saturated environment. We will then delve into practical strategies for establishing and strengthening our analog anchors, redefining productivity away from the glow of monitors, and nurturing communities in the flesh.

The digital tide is a marvel of our times, but let us not be swept away. Instead, let us learn to stand firm, rooted in the rich soil of real-world experiences, even as we navigate the digital waves. Welcome to "Analog Anchors: Grounding Ourselves in the Digital Tide." Welcome to the beginning of your balanced future.

And so we must always ask ourselves: what will be your anchor?

1

Navigating the Digital Deluge

The History of Digital Overwhelm

In the annals of human innovation, the advent of digital technology stands out as a revolution that reshaped the world. To understand our current state of digital overwhelm, we must journey back to the origins of this transformation and observe how each wave of advancement brought us to where we are today.

Our story begins with the birth of the internet—a network of computers originally designed to share information across vast distances. The internet was a marvel, a digital frontier that promised limitless knowledge at our fingertips. It was a time of digital optimism, where the ping of a dial-up modem was a clarion call to new discoveries.

As personal computers found their way into homes and offices, they carried with them the promise of increased efficiency and productivity. Software became more sophisticated, and tasks that once required painstaking manual effort were now accomplished with a few clicks. Yet, with every program and platform, our screens became busier, our workdays longer, and our interactions with the digital world more complex.

Email was one of the first truly revolutionary internet applications, a digital missive that could be sent at nearly the speed of light. Inboxes became the new mailboxes, filled not just with personal notes but with newsletters, promotions, and an ever-growing list of professional obligations. The novelty of receiving an email gave way to the stress of managing hundreds. The simplicity of communication became the complexity of constant contact.

The launch of the smartphone was a turning point, unmooring digital access from the desktop and putting it into our pockets. Connectivity became constant, and with it, the barriers between work, home, and play blurred. Smartphones brought with them an ecosystem of apps for every conceivable purpose, each vying for our attention, each notification a drop in the deluge.

Social media platforms connected billions of lives, giving everyone a voice and a virtual space to share their stories. But this democratization of discourse also meant an inundation of content—never-ending feeds of updates, photos, and videos, demanding our attention and contributing to a sense of social overload.

The digital age has turned information scarcity into surplus. Where we once thirsted for knowledge, we now find ourselves drowning in data. The abundance that promised to free our minds has, in many instances, fettered them to a never-ending scroll, a constant chase for the latest update, the freshest content.

This historical journey brings us to our current state: a paradox where abundance leads to deficit—deficits of time, attention, and ultimately, well-being. The digital tools designed to streamline life have often cluttered it, turning the joy of connectivity into a juggling act of digital demands.

Understanding the history of our digital overwhelm is the first step towards regaining control. It gives context to our struggle and highlights the importance of developing strategies to manage the information excess. As we delve further into the concept of Analog Anchors, we will explore how we can tether ourselves to the physical world, finding balance in an age of digital extremes.

From Aid to Addiction: Technology's Slippery Slope

In the narrative of our digital lives, what began as an aid has, for many, morphed into an addiction. It's a tale of gradual entanglement in the very tools that promised liberation.

At the core of technology's addictive nature is its ability to tap into the brain's reward system. Each notification, like, or retweet triggers a release of dopamine, a neurotransmitter associated with pleasure. This intermittent reinforcement—the unpredictable yet frequent rewards— ensnares us in a cycle of anticipation and gratification that can be hard to break.

The smartphone embodies this cycle, always promising something new. It's a portal to an endless stream of stimuli, where the potential for a rewarding experience is just a swipe away. This perpetual novelty keeps the brain engaged in a state of heightened alertness, always seeking the next digital hit.

The design elements of technology also play a critical role in its addictive potential. Features such as infinite scrolling, push notifications, and auto-play videos are crafted to capture and keep our attention. Tech companies deploy armies of designers and psychologists who understand human behavior deeply and use this knowledge to increase engagement, often prioritizing it over user well-being.

The colors, sounds, and interactions of our devices and apps are fine-tuned to maximize their allure. The bright red notifications, the satisfying 'ping' of a new message—these are not arbitrary design choices. They are the result of meticulous engineering aimed at increasing time spent on the device.

The convenience afforded by technology comes at a price. The always-on culture it fosters has blurred the lines between work and rest, public and private, leading to a state of continuous partial attention. We're constantly reachable, and therefore, we're never truly off duty. This erosion of boundaries contributes to stress, burnout, and a decrease in the quality of our personal relationships.

Despite being more connected than ever before, many report feeling lonelier. Social media can create an illusion of connection that lacks the depth and fulfillment of face-to-face interactions. We curate our lives, presenting a highlight reel that can lead to comparisons and a sense of inadequacy, feeding a cycle of anxiety and compulsive use.

The journey from aid to addiction is not one of sudden descent but a gradual, almost imperceptible slide. It's not the technology itself that's inherently harmful; it's the way we've come to use it—and the way it uses us—that's cause for concern. Recognizing this is the first step in recalibrating our relationship with digital tools, allowing them to serve us rather than enslave us.

In the following chapters, we will explore how we might counteract this trend, setting deliberate intentions for our technology use and establishing Analog Anchors to keep us grounded in the tangible world. By doing so, we aim to turn the tide, reclaiming control from the grasp of digital addiction.

The Consequences of the Deluge

The digital deluge has reshaped the landscape of our daily lives. It's not just the volume of information but the way it scatters our attention and intentions, leaving a unique footprint on our personal well-being, professional lives, and society at large.

On a personal level, the constant barrage of information and the compulsion to remain digitally connected can lead to a sense of overload and fatigue. The promise of a more manageable life, facilitated by digital tools, often feels betrayed. Many individuals report feelings of anxiety and depression linked to digital overuse, finding themselves caught in the comparison trap on social media or struggling to keep up with the relentless pace of online communication.

The irony is stark: in an age designed for connectivity, individuals report higher levels of loneliness. The superficial interactions offered by digital communication pale in comparison to the nuanced and fulfilling experience of face-to-face interactions. Relationships, mediated by screens, can lack the depth and authenticity that come from being physically present with others.

Professionally, the digital deluge has transformed the workday, stretching it to all hours and infringing upon what was once personal time. The expectation to be always available has eroded work-life boundaries, contributing to burnout and reducing overall job satisfaction. Moreover, the multitasking demanded by constant digital interruptions can undermine productivity and the quality of work, contradicting the efficiency that technology was supposed to enhance.

Societally, the digital deluge has shifted the way communities form, interact, and function. There is a decline in civic engagement and face-to-face social activities, replaced by online communities that, while valuable, often foster echo chambers rather than diverse interactions. The speed and anonymity of online communication can also amplify negative behaviors, such as bullying and misinformation, impacting societal cohesion and trust.

This paradox of plenty—endless information but a scarcity of meaning and connection—raises important questions about how we structure our lives around digital technology. We've become excellent at broadcasting ourselves, yet the skills of listening and being present are at risk of atrophy. The deluge, with its constant flow of stimuli, demands a response, but not all responses are equal. Depth, reflection, and understanding often drown in the shallows of quick digital exchanges.

The following chapters will explore ways to navigate these challenges, looking at strategies to mitigate the negative impacts of the digital delague. We will consider how Analog Anchors can serve as lifelines, helping us reclaim the time and space needed for a fulfilling and balanced existence amidst the ceaseless digital currents.

Charting a Course Through the Waters

In facing the rough waters of the digital age, we must become adept navigators, aware of the currents and undercurrents that influence our journey. The strategies outlined in this section are like navigational tools, guiding us to engage with technology in a way that serves our deepest needs and values.

The first step in navigation is to understand the currents—our digital consumption patterns. Just as sailors once used the stars to orient themselves, we can use tools and apps to monitor our digital usage. Awareness is pivotal; by tracking the time spent on devices, the nature of our interactions, and the emotional states associated with them, we can begin to discern patterns. This understanding allows us to make informed decisions about our digital behavior.

To chart a course through these waters, we must set boundaries. These can take many forms: designated tech-free hours, limiting certain apps to specific times of the day, or creating tech-free zones in our homes. Setting limits on digital consumption is not about renunciation but about creating space for focused work, meaningful interactions, and personal reflection.

With an understanding of our digital patterns and boundaries in place, we can prioritize our engagements. This involves conscious choices about which digital interactions add value to our lives and which detract from it. It's about quality over quantity, choosing depth and relevance over the superficial and distracting.

Technology itself can be a tool for navigation. There are apps designed to limit usage, filter content, and block distractions. Techniques such as batching email or using social media intentionally, rather than reactively, can also serve as rudders, keeping us on course.

Despite our best efforts, there will be times when we're caught in a squall of digital demands. Developing resilience is key—knowing when to disconnect entirely and weather the storm in a quiet harbor. This may involve short digital detoxes or simply more stringent adherence to our established boundaries during times of high stress.

As we chart our individual courses, we contribute to a collective rethinking of the role of technology in our lives. By sharing strategies and supporting each other's journeys, we can navigate toward a horizon where technology serves humanity's well-being, rather than detracts from it. The chapters ahead will build upon these strategies, introducing the concept of Analog Anchors as a means to maintain the course we've set and to stay true to the compass of our values.

The Digital Compass: Identifying True North

In the vast sea of digital information, it's easy to drift off course. A digital compass, our core values and intentions, can guide us through the waters, helping us to discern the essential from the expendable.

The first step in crafting a digital compass is to define what matters most. These values—whether they be connection, creativity, knowledge, or productivity—act as the cardinal points that guide our digital engagement. When we're clear about what we value, we can align our online behavior with these principles.

With our values as a guide, we can set our bearings by approaching digital spaces with intentionality. This means being proactive about how we use technology, rather than reactive to its demands. Before opening an app or responding to a notification, we pause to ask whether this action aligns with our values, serving as a checkpoint to keep us on course.

In an environment saturated with information, the skill of selective attention becomes vital. This involves distinguishing between the signal—content that is meaningful and useful—and the noise—distracting or irrelevant information. By applying our digital compass, we can steer toward the signal, minimizing the time and energy we lose to the noise.

Every click, swipe, or tap is a choice. By using our digital compass, we make these choices consciously, selecting pathways that lead us toward fulfillment and growth. This may mean curating our social media feeds to reflect our interests, choosing quality news sources, or engaging with online communities that share our values.

As we journey through the digital world, our compass requires regular calibration. Our values may shift, or the digital landscape may change. Periodic reevaluation ensures that our compass remains true, guiding us toward our own True North despite the changing tides.

By establishing and adhering to a digital compass, we claim the power to navigate the digital realm according to our deepest principles. It's a tool for maintaining direction in a world that often feels directionless, enabling us to select the engagements that will enrich our lives and bypass those that will not. As we continue to explore the theme of Analog Anchors in the chapters that follow, this compass will be indispensable in helping us anchor our digital habits to the bedrock of our most cherished values.

2

Our Minds in the Machine

As the dawn of the digital age breaks, it's not just the world around us that has transformed; the very fabric of our mental processes has been interfaced with the circuitry of modern technology. In the palm of our hands, we hold devices with the power to access all human knowledge, to connect with others across the globe, and to manage our lives with unparalleled convenience. Yet, with these profound capabilities comes a subtle reprogramming of our cognition and affect—the essence of our mental and emotional selves.

We find ourselves at a critical juncture where the line between user and tool blurs. Smartphones, computers, and wearables are no longer mere extensions of our physical selves but have become intertwined with the way we think, feel, and perceive the world. These devices and platforms, designed to leverage human psychology for engagement and retention, now have a reciprocal effect, shaping the very psychology they sought to harness.

In this chapter, we explore the complex interplay between human cognition and digital tools. We'll unravel the threads of how constant connectivity is reshaping our attention spans, how the vastness of the internet is impacting our memory, and how the personalized algorithms of our feeds are influencing our emotions and beliefs. As we navigate through digital landscapes, our neural pathways are trodden into new patterns, reflecting the rhythms and pulses of online life.

But what does this mean for the core of our humanity? How do we preserve the essence of what it means to be human when our minds are so deeply enmeshed with machines? This is not a journey into a dystopian future but an exploration of the present reality—a reality where mindfulness and technology must coexist and where the autonomy of the human spirit must be vigilantly safeguarded against the seductive lure of digital omnipresence.

This chapter will not only describe the phenomenon but also initiate a conversation about balance. It's a call to redefine the boundaries between our mental space and the digital world, ensuring that as we use these extraordinary tools, we do not lose sight of the extraordinary beings we are—capable of creativity, deep thought, and profound emotion, independent of the glowing screens that have become our constant companions.

As we delve deeper into the cognitive and emotional effects of our digital engagements, we invite you to pause and reflect. In the subsequent sections, we will lay bare the challenges and offer strategies to foster a harmony between our minds and the machines that have become an inextricable part of our lives. This is not a path of rejection but one of recognition and recalibration, where we learn to coexist with technology without letting it define us.

Cognitive Echoes: How Technology Mimics the Mind

In the intricate dance between the human mind and digital technology, there is a mirroring effect where each reflects and shapes the other in a continuous feedback loop. In the digital environments where we spend increasing portions of our lives, the very architecture is crafted to mimic and interact with our cognitive functions. This section delves into how these environments are designed with the human mind in mind, and how, in turn, they begin to reshape the very thought processes that they emulate.

I. MIRRORING NEURONS: THE DESIGN OF DIGITAL SPACES

Digital spaces are not arbitrary but are carefully engineered to resonate with our innate cognitive preferences. Interfaces leverage the same neural pathways that we use for physical interaction, creating intuitive experiences that feel "natural" to us. From the swipe of a screen to the structure of menus and options, technology is a mirror that reflects our ways of understanding and engaging with the world.

II. COGNITIVE RESONANCE: DESIGN PRINCIPLES THAT ENGAGE

The principles of digital design often capitalize on cognitive biases and heuristics. The 'endless scroll' takes advantage of our tendency for curiosity and the 'fear of missing out,' while notifications and likes tap into our need for social validation. These design choices create a resonance with our cognitive tendencies, making digital platforms incredibly sticky and compelling.

III. FEEDBACK LOOPS: THE RECIPROCAL INFLUENCE ON THOUGHT

As we interact with digital environments, there's a subtle co-evolution occurring. Our cognitive patterns, like pathways in a forest, become more pronounced with use. Simultaneously, we begin to think and expect outcomes in ways that align with the digital logic we engage with daily. Our problem-solving, decision-making, and even creative thinking are, to an extent, being modeled after the algorithms and processes that underpin our favorite apps and platforms.

IV. THE ECHOING MIND: COGNITION ALTERED

Through prolonged engagement with these environments, our cognition begins to echo the structures and functions of the digital tools we use. Some scholars suggest that the neuroplasticity of our brains allows them to reshape in response to these interactions. The question then arises: what are the long-term cognitive consequences of living in a world designed to reflect and engage our minds in such a targeted way?

Understanding this cognitive mirroring is crucial not only for designers and developers but for users who wish to engage with technology mindfully. By recognizing the ways in which digital environments are modeled after and influence our cognitive processes, we can take steps to ensure that our engagement strengthens rather than diminishes our mental faculties. As we progress through the chapters, we will explore strategies to mitigate the risks and enhance the benefits of our inevitable interaction with digital mirrors.

The Attention Economy: Mining Minds for Time

In the digital age, the adage "time is money" has never been more literal. Human attention has become the new currency, with companies vying for every possible moment of our gaze and engagement. This section investigates how the economics of attention operates and the psychological toll it takes on individuals who find themselves as the product in a market that trades in the currency of human focus.

I. ATTENTION AS COMMODITY: THE NEW CURRENCY

We live in an economy where businesses are built on the capture and retention of human attention. This isn't just about the time spent on a platform but about how that time translates into data, influence, and ultimately, profit. As users, our clicks, views, and time spent are meticulously tracked, packaged, and sold to the highest bidder in the form of targeted advertising and predictive analytics.

II. THE MARKET OF MINDS: BUSINESS MODELS FOR ENGAGEMENT

Digital platforms are intricately designed to keep us engaged for as long as possible. From social media to news outlets, the strategies for capturing attention are sophisticated and ever-evolving. The 'pull-to-refresh' feature, video autoplay, and personalized content feeds are not merely convenient features but deliberate designs to ensure that our time on the platform maximizes their revenue.

III. PSYCHOLOGICAL IMPACT: THE COST OF CONSTANT ENGAGEMENT

This relentless demand for our attention comes with a psychological cost. The human brain is not wired for the continuous task-switching and overstimulation that the attention economy demands. This can lead to a scattered focus, reduced productivity, and a diminished capacity for deep, reflective thought. Moreover, the constant bombardment of information and stimuli can contribute to stress, anxiety, and a pervasive sense of overwhelm.

IV. ATTENTION, INTERRUPTED: FRAGMENTING OUR MENTAL CONTINUITY

Our mental continuity is disrupted as we succumb to the siren call of notifications and alerts. Each interruption may seem minor, but cumulatively they fragment our attention span, making sustained concentration more difficult. The design of digital technology taps into the brain's reward system, keeping us in a state of anticipatory dopamine-driven loops, which can be both exhausting and addictive.

V. RECLAIMING FOCUS: STRATEGIES FOR SELF-DEFENSE

As the battle for our attention intensifies, it becomes crucial to develop personal strategies to defend our focus. This can include setting boundaries around technology use, curating notifications, and consciously designing our digital environment to minimize distractions.

To navigate the attention economy without losing ourselves to it, we must become aware of the forces at play and actively choose how we engage with digital media. The strategies discussed later in this book aim to empower readers to reclaim their attention and focus, ensuring that our minds remain our own, not just another commodity to be mined for time.

Digital Distractions: Fragmenting Our Focus

In this age of information surplus, our ability to concentrate is being challenged by a barrage of digital distractions. Each ping, beep, and flash from our devices fractures our focus, pulling us away from the task at hand. This section delves into the nature of these interruptions, their impact on our cognitive capabilities, and the erosion of our capacity for deep thought.

I. THE FRAGMENTATION OF ATTENTION

Digital distractions are omnipresent. The average smartphone user is interrupted by notifications many times a day, each one an invitation to divert their attention. These disruptions are not just momentary; they have a ripple effect, fragmenting our focus and making it increasingly difficult to return to a state of concentrated attention.

II. THE SCIENCE OF DISTRACTION

Neuroscientific research shows that it can take significantly longer to refocus on a task after being distracted. Each interruption may seem trivial, but cumulatively, they add up to a substantial cognitive load, reducing our mental resources available for complex thought and problem-solving.

III. DEEP THOUGHT IN SHALLOW STREAMS

The shallow, rapid streams of information that flow from our screens are at odds with the deep, slow-moving rivers of thought required for complex analysis and creativity. The environment of instant gratification and rapid content consumption actively works against the mental discipline needed for deep work.

IV. THE COST OF CONSTANT CONNECTIVITY

Being 'always-on' and responsive to the digital world can lead to a chronic state of vigilance, which is mentally taxing and can inhibit the restorative mental states necessary for deep thought. The psychological impacts range from decreased memory retention to increased anxiety and a pervasive sense that one can never fully disengage or relax.

V. REWIRING FOR DEPTH: CULTIVATING CONCENTRATION

Despite the challenges, we are not helpless. This section will explore strategies to cultivate concentration and protect our cognitive environment. By deliberately managing our digital interactions, we can rewire our habits toward more sustained, meaningful engagements with tasks and reduce the cognitive cost of digital distractions.

The long-term effects of a distracted mind can be profound, but so too can be the benefits of cultivating a focused one. By understanding the mechanics of digital distractions and their impact on our focus, we can begin to implement measures to preserve our cognitive space, allowing for deeper engagement with our work, our passions, and our lives. The remainder of the book will serve as a guide for those looking to forge paths of concentration in the fragmented landscape of the digital world.

Emotional Algorithms: When Technology Knows How We Feel

In the labyrinth of digital interaction, algorithms are no longer mere passive tools; they have evolved to read, predict, and sometimes even manipulate our emotional states. This section scrutinizes the sophistication with which technology now approaches our feelings and the ramifications for personal emotional autonomy.

I. DECODING EMOTIONS: THE ALGORITHMIC MIRROR

Tech companies have developed algorithms sophisticated enough to decode human emotions. Through the analysis of data such as facial expressions, voice intonations, and interaction patterns, these algorithms can infer our mood and emotional states with unnerving accuracy. These emotional algorithms are the mirrors reflecting not just our faces, but the contours of our inner selves.

II. SENTIMENT ANALYSIS: THE PULSE OF EMOTION

Sentiment analysis is a tool that mines text for emotional subtext, allowing companies to gauge reactions to products, services, or content. This powerful tool transforms casual tweets, comments, and reviews into valuable insights into collective emotional responses, further blurring the line between public and private sentiment.

III. RESPONSIVE TECHNOLOGY: ADAPTING TO MOODS

Responsive technologies adjust what we see online based on inferred emotional states, shaping our digital experiences to our moods. The music streaming service that curates playlists to our emotions, or the social platform that alters our feed when we seem down, may offer comfort, but at the price of our emotional independence and unpredictability.

IV. THE MANIPULATION OF MOOD: THE POWER OF SUGGESTION

The power to discern emotion can easily slide into the power to influence it. Advertisements and content are no longer just targeted based on demographics or interests but are becoming tailored to resonate with our current emotional state, exploiting moments of vulnerability or happiness to drive engagement or consumption.

V. PRESERVING EMOTIONAL AUTONOMY

With the increasing encroachment of algorithms into our emotional lives, it's imperative to understand and set boundaries for these technologies. Strategies for preserving emotional autonomy in the face of emotionally aware algorithms will be essential for maintaining personal well-being and agency.

The emerging era of emotional algorithms presents profound ethical and personal challenges. As we peel back the layers of how technology interfaces with our emotions, it becomes clear that the stewardship of our emotional lives is a new frontier in the quest for digital well-being. The book's later sections will provide guidance on navigating this complex and emotionally charged terrain, ensuring that our feelings remain our own, and not another data point to be exploited.

Memory in the Age of Google: Outsourcing the Mind

In this modern tapestry of terabytes and tech, our memories are becoming intertwined with digital databases. This chapter delves deep into the implications of our growing reliance on technology for memory storage and retrieval, examining how this symbiosis is reshaping our mental capacities and the very way we remember.

I. THE EXTERNALIZATION OF MEMORY

As we increasingly outsource memory to digital devices, we must question the impact on our neural processes. Search engines, cloud storage, and smartphones serve as external hard drives for our brains, holding information that we once committed to memory. This section investigates the shift from internal memory processes to an external, digital-based recall system.

II. GOOGLE EFFECT: THE DIMINISHING NEED FOR RECALL

The phenomenon known as the "Google Effect" refers to the tendency to forget information that can be easily found online. With answers always a few keystrokes away, the need to remember has diminished, and with it, our practice of the art of memory. We explore the psychological and cognitive science behind this effect and its broader implications for learning and cognition.

III. THE PLASTICITY OF THE BRAIN: ADAPTING TO TECHNOLOGICAL CRUTCHES

Human memory is malleable, with the brain capable of reorganizing itself in response to changes in behavior and environment—a concept known as neuroplasticity. This section covers how the brain adapts to the reliance on technology, potentially weakening our natural memory systems, while possibly enhancing our skills in navigating and manipulating information in the digital realm.

IV. COGNITIVE CONSEQUENCES: THE LONG-TERM EFFECTS

This reliance on digital tools for memory poses questions about the long-term cognitive consequences. Are we hindering our ability to perform complex tasks that require the integration of various pieces of remembered information? Or is this shift simply a natural evolution of our cognitive processes, comparable to the way written language changed our memory?

V. MEMORY AND IDENTITY: THE PERSONAL NARRATIVE

Memory is fundamental to our sense of self. It is the bedrock upon which our personal narrative is built. By entrusting our memories to digital devices, we may be altering the way we construct our identities and perceive our past. This section reflects on how the digital age is changing the narrative structure of our lives and the way we relate to our personal histories.

VI. RETAINING MEMORY FITNESS: MENTAL AGILITY IN THE DIGITAL ERA

Just as physical fitness requires regular exercise, memory fitness benefits from consistent mental challenges. We'll explore techniques and habits that can help maintain and improve memory in a world where technology remembers for us, from mnemonic devices to the practice of deliberate recall and mindfulness.

Our journey through the landscape of memory in the digital age concludes with a balanced perspective. While the conveniences of technology are undeniable, this chapter underlines the importance of maintaining mental resilience through active engagement with our memory processes. It sets the stage for later discussions on creating a harmonious relationship with technology—one that supports our cognitive well-being and enriches our human experience.

The Illusion of Multitasking: Juggling Digital Tasks

In this hyper-connected digital age, multitasking is often heralded as a virtue, a necessary skill for navigating the deluge of demands on our attention. However, this chapter peels back the veneer of multitasking to reveal the cognitive illusions and costs beneath.

I. THE MYTH OF MULTITASKING

Contrary to popular belief, what we call multitasking is often rapid task-switching. The human brain is not wired to focus on multiple complex tasks simultaneously. This section delves into the neuroscience behind our focus and how our belief in our multitasking abilities is at odds with reality.

II. COGNITIVE LOAD AND TASK SWITCHING

Each task we undertake requires a certain amount of cognitive resources. Switching between tasks not only depletes these resources more quickly but also increases the time taken to complete each task. We explore how this cognitive load diminishes our efficiency and accuracy, leading to a decrease in overall productivity.

III. THE COST OF CONTEXT SWITCHING

Context switching refers to the mental adjustment required when shifting from one task to another. This adjustment period can cause a cognitive "lag" that reduces our ability to perform effectively. This section examines the implications of context switching, especially when involving complex or creative tasks.

IV. QUALITY OF WORK AND DEPTH OF ENGAGEMENT

Multitasking often leads to surface-level engagement with tasks, preventing deep immersion and undermining the quality of our work. Here, we reflect on how the constant juggling of digital tasks impacts the depth of our engagement with work, hindering our ability to perform deep work and produce high-quality outcomes.

V. RECLAIMING SINGULAR FOCUS

Acknowledging the limitations of multitasking, this section presents strategies for fostering a singular focus. From techniques like time-blocking and the Pomodoro Technique to setting up a distraction-free environment, we look at ways to minimize the need for task-switching and cultivate deep, sustained attention.

As we unravel the multitasking myth, it becomes evident that embracing a monotasking mindset is not regressive but rather a progressive step towards harnessing the full potential of our cognitive abilities. This chapter challenges readers to rethink their digital work habits, advocating for a more intentional and focused approach to task management in the digital landscape.

The book continues to build on these principles, ultimately guiding readers toward a philosophy of digital engagement that emphasizes quality over quantity, depth over breadth, and ultimately, human cognitive health over digital dexterity.

Echo Chambers and Filter Bubbles: The Personalization Trap

In this hyper-connected digital age, multitasking is often heralded as a virtue, a necessary skill for navigating the deluge of demands on our attention. However, this chapter peels back the veneer of multitasking to reveal the cognitive illusions and costs beneath.

I. THE MYTH OF MULTITASKING

Contrary to popular belief, what we call multitasking is often rapid task-switching. The human brain is not wired to focus on multiple complex tasks simultaneously. This section delves into the neuroscience behind our focus and how our belief in our multitasking abilities is at odds with reality.

II. COGNITIVE LOAD AND TASK SWITCHING

Each task we undertake requires a certain amount of cognitive resources. Switching between tasks not only depletes these resources more quickly but also increases the time taken to complete each task. We explore how this cognitive load diminishes our efficiency and accuracy, leading to a decrease in overall productivity.

III. THE COST OF CONTEXT SWITCHING

Context switching refers to the mental adjustment required when shifting from one task to another. This adjustment period can cause a cognitive "lag" that reduces our ability to perform effectively. This section examines the implications of context switching, especially when involving complex or creative tasks.

iv. Quality of Work and Depth of Engagement

Multitasking often leads to surface-level engagement with tasks, preventing deep immersion and undermining the quality of our work. Here, we reflect on how the constant juggling of digital tasks impacts the depth of our engagement with work, hindering our ability to perform deep work and produce high-quality outcomes.

V. RECLAIMING SINGULAR FOCUS

Acknowledging the limitations of multitasking, this section presents strategies for fostering a singular focus. From techniques like time-blocking and the Pomodoro Technique to setting up a distraction-free environment, we look at ways to minimize the need for task-switching and cultivate deep, sustained attention.

As we unravel the multitasking myth, it becomes evident that embracing a monotasking mindset is not regressive but rather a progressive step towards harnessing the full potential of our cognitive abilities. This chapter challenges readers to rethink their digital work habits, advocating for a more intentional and focused approach to task management in the digital landscape.

The book continues to build on these principles, ultimately guiding readers toward a philosophy of digital engagement that emphasizes quality over quantity, depth over breadth, and ultimately, human cognitive health over digital dexterity.

The Paradox of Choice: Overwhelmed in a Sea of Options

As digital consumers, we are confronted with an endless array of choices, from streaming videos and music to purchasing goods, reading news, and even dating. While this abundance might seem advantageous, this chapter explores how an excess of options can paradoxically lead to decision fatigue, overwhelm, and a pervasive dissatisfaction.

I. UNDERSTANDING THE PARADOX

Initially, we unpack the paradox itself: the concept that having many options can lead to worse decisions, or the inability to make a decision at all. The paradox of choice challenges the traditional notion that more is better, suggesting that there can be a point of diminishing returns when it comes to options.

II. ANALYSIS OF CHOICE OVERLOAD

Choice overload occurs when the cognitive burden of weighing options exceeds the benefits of the choice itself. This section delves into the psychological strain caused by the plethora of choices in the digital sphere, from minor daily decisions like what to watch on Netflix, to significant life decisions facilitated by digital means.

III. THE TYRANNY OF SMALL DECISIONS

The cumulative effect of making numerous inconsequential decisions can sap our energy and willpower, leaving us less capable of making more substantial decisions. This phenomenon, known as the tyranny of small decisions, is amplified in the digital world where micro-decisions are constant.

IV. MAXIMIZERS VS. SATISFICERS

The chapter then introduces two types of decision-makers: maximizers, who seek out all possible options to make the best decision, and satisficers, who aim for "good enough" rather than the best. We explore how the digital age is pushing more people towards maximization and the stress that accompanies this shift.

V. REDUCING SATISFACTION AND WELL-BEING

The abundance of choice can lead to increased anxiety, regret, and even depression. We examine how the pressure to make the 'right' choice, coupled with the fear of missing out (FOMO), undermines our satisfaction and well-being.

VI. STRATEGIES FOR SIMPLIFYING CHOICES

Finally, we present strategies for managing the paradox of choice in the digital environment. From setting personal guidelines and limits to embracing the art of satisficing, we provide actionable advice for reducing the stress associated with digital decision-making.

In closing, the chapter brings us full circle to the theme of digital simplicity. It suggests that by consciously limiting our options, we can alleviate the pressure of the paradox of choice, leading to greater satisfaction and a more serene digital life. The paradox of choice serves as a compelling argument for the principles of digital minimalism, where less is indeed more, and where the freedom from choice can be liberating and lead to a more focused and fulfilling digital existence.

Cyberpsychology: The New Terrain of Mental Health

Cyberpsychology, an emergent field at the intersection of psychology and technology, scrutinizes how digital spaces influence human behavior and mental health. This chapter contemplates the myriad ways in which our online lives intersect with our psychological well-being, casting light on the need for greater awareness and new approaches to mental health in the digital age.

I. FOUNDATIONS OF CYBERPSYCHOLOGY

We begin by laying the groundwork, defining cyberpsychology and explaining its significance. By exploring its origins and current reach, we frame the conversation around the impact of the digital world on the human psyche.

II. IDENTITY AND SELF-ESTEEM ONLINE

Digital platforms present novel ways of expressing and experimenting with identity, impacting self-esteem and self-perception. This section examines how social media, online gaming, and virtual realities contribute to the construction of self-identity and the effects on individual self-esteem.

III. ONLINE INTERACTIONS AND MENTAL WELL-BEING

Human connections have evolved with online interactions, forums, and social networking sites. We delve into how these virtual relationships affect our mental well-being, considering both the supportive communities and the negative effects of online hostility, cyberbullying, and social isolation.

IV. ADDICTION AND COMPULSION IN THE DIGITAL SPHERE

The addictive nature of digital engagement, from social media to video games, is explored, highlighting the characteristics that make digital environments ripe for compulsive behaviors. We look at how the design of digital products can encourage habitual use and the implications for mental health.

V. THE IMPACT OF DIGITAL STRESSORS

Cyberpsychology also examines the stress and anxiety that can stem from constant connectivity and the pressure to maintain a digital presence. This section considers the role of digital stressors in contemporary life, such as the expectation of instant communication and the burden of information overload.

VI. THERAPEUTIC INTERVENTIONS AND DIGITAL DETOXES

As recognition of these issues grows, so too do the therapeutic interventions aimed at mitigating them. We discuss the rise of digital detoxes, mindfulness practices, and therapy that specifically addresses digital-related stressors, considering the effectiveness and limitations of these approaches.

VII. EMERGING TRENDS AND FUTURE DIRECTIONS

This chapter concludes with a forward-looking perspective on the trends shaping cyberpsychology, such as the increasing use of digital technology in therapeutic settings and the development of preventive measures to maintain mental health in a digital world.

The narrative closes with a call to integrate the principles of cyberpsychology into everyday digital use. By understanding the psychological impact of our online behavior, we can chart a course towards a healthier digital existence, one that respects our mental health and nurtures our well-being amidst the pervasive influence of technology. The takeaway is a balanced view of digital engagement as a potent tool for good when used mindfully and a potential risk when mismanaged.

As we close this exploratory journey into the intricate dance between our mental landscapes and the pervasive digital technologies that surround us, we come away with a deeper awareness of the ties that bind us to our devices—and the strings we can pull to maintain our autonomy.

The insights gleaned from the various chapters form a mosaic of understanding. We've examined the cognitive echoes and the way technology is both a mirror and a molder of our minds. We've delved into the attention economy, understanding that our mental focus is the new currency in a marketplace that thrives on our engagement. We've confronted the ways in which digital distractions fragment our thought processes, how algorithms play to our emotions, and the startling implications of our outsourced memories.

Furthermore, we've debunked the myth of multitasking, peered into the echo chambers and filter bubbles that shape our perceptions, and grappled with the paradox of choice that overwhelms our decision-making capacities. Finally, we've touched upon the emerging field of cyberpsychology and its role in mental health.

The next steps involve turning this understanding into action. It's about asserting control over our digital interactions, carving out spaces for reflection, and setting boundaries that prioritize our mental well-being. The strategies that will be presented aim to empower us to resist the pull of convenience and immediacy that digital technologies offer, advocating for a more deliberate and intentional approach to their use.

Beyond reclaiming our time and attention, we need to foster resilience in our cognitive and emotional realms. This means engaging in practices that bolster our concentration, enhance our memory, and enrich our emotional intelligence. By doing so, we shore up our defenses against the relentless tide of the digital onslaught.

It's time to anchor ourselves in principles that transcend the digital tide. By committing to the practices outlined in the forthcoming sections, we can navigate the digital age not as passive consumers, but as active and mindful participants. In doing so, we harness the true potential of our technologies while securing the sanctity of our mental spaces.

3

Analog Anchors Defined

In the swift currents of a digital-centric society, where our days are often punctuated by the pings and buzzes of notifications, the concept of 'Analog Anchors' emerges as a beacon of balance. These Anchors are not mere nostalgic relics but essential practices and habits that root us firmly in the physical world. Their role is not to reject the digital but to offer a counterweight, a grounding force amidst the often intangible and transient nature of our online existences.

Analog Anchors hark back to a time when life's rhythms were dictated by nature and human interaction, rather than algorithms and network connectivity. They remind us that, before our pockets vibrated with every email, like, or share, we found joy and meaning in the pages of books, the warmth of in-person conversations, and the simple solitude of our own thoughts. These practices, be they the morning ritual of brewing coffee without the glare of a screen, or the evening stroll detached from the digital tether, serve as lifelines back to the essence of human experience.

In this chapter, we will define what constitutes an Analog Anchor, from the simplicity of handwritten letters to the complexity of gardening, where we nurture life with our hands and not through a keyboard. We will explore why these practices are more than just activities; they are statements of intent, deliberate choices that reaffirm our sovereignty over our attention and time.

We will also investigate why these Anchors are crucial for our well-being. The digital world, with all its benefits, often casts a shadow of constant availability and endless information that can lead to a sense of dislocation from our environment and ourselves. Analog Anchors pull us back from the precipice of this digital abyss, offering solace in the tactile and the tangible.

Moreover, these Anchors are the foundation upon which a more intentional lifestyle can be built. In a world where every second can be monetized, every interaction analyzed for engagement, choosing to engage in analog activities is a radical act of self-preservation and authenticity. It's a way to assert that not all our moments need to be shared, optimized, or monetized, that some can simply be lived and enjoyed.

As we dive into the specifics of Analog Anchors, we will learn how they serve not just as a toolkit for personal equilibrium but as signposts for a community and culture that values depth over distraction, connection over mere connectivity, and the enduring over the ephemeral. They are not a step backwards but a path forward to a lifestyle that champions balance, contentment, and true engagement with the world around us.

The Essence of Analog Anchors

At the heart of the concept of Analog Anchors lies the recognition of activities and habits that foster a profound connection with the tangible, the real, the non-digitally mediated facets of life. These anchors are not just actions but experiences deeply rooted in the physical world, which engage our senses and our being in ways that pixels and screens cannot replicate. They are the physical books whose pages we turn, the ink smudges they leave on our fingers, the conversations where we perceive the subtle inflections of voice and the micro-expressions that flicker across faces, the immersive quietude of nature where the only timeline to scroll through is the slow progression of the sun across the sky.

i. Physical Books and the Act of Reading

Analog Anchors in reading involve the sensory experience of holding a book, feeling the weight of it in your hands, and the sound of a page turning. It's a ritual that includes marking a page with a beloved bookmark, the smell of the paper, and the quiet focus that comes from being immersed in a narrative without the possibility of a notification pulling you away.

ii. Conversations Without Screens

Face-to-face conversations as Analog Anchors provide a level of connection and understanding that is often diminished or distorted by digital communication. It's in these interactions that we find nuances and meanings, understanding and empathy, forged in the crucible of eye contact, body language, and shared silences.

iii. Nature as an Anchor

Spending time in nature — whether it be tending a garden, walking in a park, or hiking through wilderness — acts as an anchor by offering a respite from the digital world. It's a place where time can slow down, where the mind can wander without being pulled back by the leash of the internet. Nature's rhythms and cycles provide a perspective that is grounding, reminding us of the world that exists beyond our constructed digital environments.

iv. Mindfulness and Movement

Mindfulness practices, yoga, martial arts, dance, or even a simple walk — these activities demand our presence, our engagement with the moment, and our bodies in a way that sitting in front of a screen does not. They become anchors by bringing our attention back to the here and now, to the breath in our lungs and the earth beneath our feet.

Analog Anchors are thus varied and personal, but they all share a common essence: they serve to ground us in our present, physical reality, providing a counterweight to the ephemeral, ever-changing digital world. They help cultivate a sense of presence, of being truly where one is, fully engaged with the environment and people around. In the following sections, we'll explore the deeper implications of these anchors and how they can be integrated into our daily lives to foster well-being, presence, and a sense of peace in an increasingly digitized world.

The Science Behind the Satisfaction

Why do we often feel a greater sense of fulfillment when we engage in tactile experiences? The answer lies not just in nostalgia or a romanticizing of the past, but in the very wiring of our brains and the evolutionary paths that have shaped our interactions with the world. This section of the chapter unpacks the psychological and neurological underpinnings that explain why activities like writing with a pen on paper or molding clay between our fingers can offer a more profound satisfaction than clicking keys and tapping screens.

i. The Tactile Brain: Touch and Neurology

Our brains have evolved to process a wide range of sensory inputs, with touch playing a fundamental role in how we learn and perceive the world. When we engage in hands-on activities, we activate various parts of our brain, including those responsible for sensory processing and motor control. The tactile feedback we receive from handling physical objects creates a rich neural experience that strengthens cognitive pathways. Research in neuroscience has shown that the act of writing by hand, for example, can lead to improved memory retention and comprehension because it involves a complex set of motor and cognitive skills.

ii. Mindfulness and Manual Activity

Tactile activities often require a level of concentration and mindfulness that digital tasks do not. The manual effort involved in creating something with your hands — be it writing, drawing, or crafting — can induce a state of flow, a term coined by psychologist Mihaly Csikszentmihalyi to describe a state of immersion and focused energy on enjoyable activities. This state not only boosts our mood but also reduces stress, providing a mental break from the incessant pace of digital consumption.

iii. The Joy of the Irreplicable

Digital experiences, while infinitely replicable, lack the unique, one-of-a-kind quality that analog experiences provide. The variability and imperfection inherent in tactile activities give rise to a sense of authenticity and personalization. This uniqueness triggers the brain's reward pathways, fostering a sense of achievement and pleasure.

iv. Artistic Engagement and Brain Plasticity

Creating art or engaging in other forms of manual creation can have regenerative and nurturing effects on the brain. These activities can stimulate neuroplasticity, the brain's ability to form new connections and pathways, which improves resilience and adaptability. Moreover, they can serve as a form of non-verbal expression that can be therapeutic and revealing, allowing for emotional release and understanding that might not be possible through digital means.

v. The Analogue as an Antidote to Overload

Finally, physical activities can serve as an antidote to cognitive overload. In a world where information comes at us in torrents, slowing down to engage with something tangible allows the brain to process at a more natural pace. The limited scope of analog tasks, in contrast to the limitless nature of digital activities, creates a natural boundary for engagement that can prevent feelings of overwhelm and burnout.

Through understanding the science behind why analog activities can feel more satisfying, we gain insights into how we can better integrate these experiences into our lives. By doing so, we cater not only to our psychological need for completion and satisfaction but also to the neurological craving for tactile, sensory-rich experiences. The following sections will explore practical ways to implement Analog Anchors in daily routines to harness these benefits for mental and emotional well-being.

Rediscovering Sensory Engagement

In a digital realm where sensory experiences are often flattened into a two-dimensional array of sight and sound, Rediscovering Sensory Engagement is about reawakening the full spectrum of human perception. This part of the chapter delves into the myriad ways we can reintegrate our senses into everyday experiences, tapping into the richness that a multi-sensory engagement with the world provides. Here we explore the importance of activities that encompass the tactile, gustatory, olfactory, visual, and auditory in a manner that goes beyond what digital interfaces can offer.

i. Touch: The Language of Texture

Touch is a language of its own, with texture, weight, temperature, and resistance telling stories that words and images cannot capture. By engaging in activities like gardening, sculpting, or even baking, we reacquaint our sense of touch with the diverse narratives of the physical world. These experiences remind us of the materiality of existence, grounding us in the reality that lies beyond the screen.

ii. Taste: The Flavor of Presence

The act of cooking and eating involves more than just taste; it is a symphony of sensory cues that create a rich, immersive experience. Digital platforms can present images of food and even attempt to describe taste, but they cannot replicate the complex flavors, the textures that dance on the tongue, or the warmth that fills the mouth. Rediscovering the joy of preparing and savoring food is an act of rebellion against the digitization of gastronomy.

iii. Smell: The Aroma of Memories

Our sense of smell is closely linked to memory and emotion, more so than any other sense. Engaging with the natural scents of the world, be it the earthiness of rain-soaked soil or the sharp tang of citrus, can evoke memories and emotions in an instant, connecting us to moments past and enriching our present experience. Digital experiences are scentless; by seeking out real-world smells, we anchor ourselves in a more authentic reality.

iv. Sight: The Palette of Reality

While digital screens can display a vast array of colors and images, they cannot replicate the full depth and detail of the world around us. Engaging in visual arts, or simply taking the time to observe the nuanced hues of a sunset, provides visual stimuli that screens cannot. The act of observing life directly also encourages us to see more mindfully, to notice the subtleties and beauty in everyday objects.

v. Hearing: The Harmony of Sounds

The sounds of the real world are rich and multidimensional, with direction, depth, and nuance. Digital audio, no matter how sophisticated, is a compressed version of this reality. Actively listening to the sounds of nature, to music played on acoustic instruments, or to the voices of loved ones without the interference of microphones and speakers, can be deeply fulfilling and grounding.

In this chapter, we not only reflect on the diminished role that our senses play in a digitally mediated life but also offer pathways to reengage them. By mindfully incorporating activities into our lives that require the use of all our senses, we can find a deeper satisfaction and a more robust presence in our daily experiences. Rediscovering Sensory Engagement is about challenging the sensory deprivation that can come with digital saturation, and about celebrating the rich tapestry of the sensory world.

Analog Anchors in a Digital Storm

The digital world can sometimes resemble a tempest: chaotic, relentless, and all-consuming. Amidst this digital storm, Analog Anchors act as a stabilizing force, providing us with a sense of calm and clarity. This section explores how we can leverage these anchors to maintain equilibrium when we are bombarded with digital noise and to find solace in the tangible world that surrounds us.

i. Seeking the Eye of the Storm: Intentional Disconnection

To establish a refuge from the digital tempest, we must first learn to disconnect intentionally. This doesn't imply a complete shunning of digital life but rather the cultivation of periods where we allow ourselves to step back and engage with the physical world. These periods of disconnection can act like the eye of a storm – a peaceful haven amidst turmoil. Whether it's a daily ritual like a morning walk without a phone or a weekly 'tech Sabbath,' these practices can provide much-needed reprieve.

ii. Physical Spaces as Sanctuaries

Our physical environment plays a crucial role in how we experience the world. By creating spaces that are devoid of digital interference – be it a reading nook, a workshop, or a garden – we can foster environments that encourage analog engagement. These sanctuaries become go-to places when the digital world becomes too intrusive, offering a literal space for grounding.

iii. Social Interactions: The Human Touch

In times of digital overload, human connections can serve as a powerful anchor. Prioritizing face-to-face interactions over digital communications can have a grounding effect, reminding us of the richness of human expression that is often lost in translation through screens. These interactions also serve as a reminder of the support systems we have around us, providing emotional stability and comfort.

iv. Hobbies and Crafts: The Art of Doing

Engaging in hobbies and crafts can be a form of active meditation, focusing the mind and keeping it anchored in the present moment. Activities like knitting, woodworking, or painting demand our full attention and engage us in a creative process that can be both calming and rewarding. The act of creating something tangible serves as a counterbalance to the ephemeral nature of the digital world.

v. Nature as a Natural Anchor

Nature has always been one of the most potent analog anchors. Immersing ourselves in the natural world allows us to experience a connection with something greater than ourselves and provides a perspective that can dwarf the importance of the digital. The rhythms of nature – the rise and fall of tides, the cycle of seasons – remind us that there is a world beyond the artificial urgency of digital notifications and deadlines.

vi. Mindful Consumption: Choosing Depth over Breadth

Finally, when we do engage with digital media, doing so mindfully can help us avoid the feeling of being swept away by the flood. This means being selective about what we consume and favoring depth over breadth – choosing long-form articles over tweets, for example, or diving into a documentary rather than scrolling through clips.

This section not only highlights the need for Analog Anchors but also offers actionable advice on integrating them into our lives. By doing so, we can find tranquility and composure, turning to these anchors to help us navigate and weather the digital storm.

The Role of Routine and Ritual

In the realm of Analog Anchors, routines and rituals play a critical role. They are not merely actions but are imbued with meaning, transforming mundane activities into touchstones of stability in our lives. This section explores how the consistent practice of routines and the observance of rituals can act as counterweights to digital disruption, providing regular moments of connection to the analog world that support our mental health and enhance our well-being.

i. Crafting Rituals for Mindful Mornings

The morning sets the tone for the entire day. Incorporating analog rituals into our morning routine—such as meditation, journaling with pen and paper, or simply enjoying a cup of coffee without the accompaniment of a screen—can anchor us in mindfulness. These practices serve as a declaration of intent for the day ahead, a statement that our attention is our own to command, not at the mercy of digital demands.

ii. Workday Rhythms: Punctuating Productivity

Even during work, where digital tools are often essential, we can establish routines that incorporate analog elements. It might involve starting each task with a handwritten plan, taking walking meetings, or setting aside technology for a midday break. These practices can punctuate our productivity with moments that remind us of the world beyond our digital devices.

iii. Analog Evenings: Unplugging to Recharge

Evenings are the perfect time to unwind and disconnect from the digital world. Rituals like preparing a meal from scratch, reading, or engaging in a hobby can help us transition from the workday's digital intensity. These activities not only provide relaxation but also serve as an investment in our skills and passions outside of the online realm.

iv. Screen-Free Sanctuaries at Home

Within our homes, we can establish certain areas as screen-free zones—sanctuaries where digital devices are not allowed. This might be the dining room during meals or the bedroom before sleep. By creating these boundaries, we cultivate spaces where routines and rituals can flourish without digital interruption, enhancing our quality of life and relationships.

v. Weekly Traditions to Look Forward To

In addition to daily routines, weekly traditions can act as anchors that root us in a sense of time and community. This could be a weekly game night, a family outdoor excursion, or volunteer work. Such traditions provide a rhythm to our lives, creating a sequence of anticipated events that offer joy and connection.

vi. Celebrating the Seasons: Annual Rituals

Beyond the daily and weekly, the observance of seasonal rituals—whether cultural, religious, or personal—connects us to a larger cycle. Engaging in annual celebrations, from holiday gatherings to seasonal festivals, ties us to the rhythms of the earth and the history of our communities.

By delineating these various layers of routines and rituals, we underscore their transformative power. These practices are not about shunning technology but about choosing when and how to engage with the digital world. They are declarations of independence, affirming that while we may operate within a digital society, we remain sovereign over our time and our attention. Through routine and ritual, we harness the power of Analog Anchors to cultivate a life of purpose, presence, and connection.

Building Resilience through Disconnection

In a society that prizes constant connectivity, the ability to disconnect is not just a luxury; it's a skill that fosters resilience. Analog Anchors are instrumental in this process. This section delves into how we can cultivate resilience through deliberate disconnection and why such practices are vital for our mental and emotional fortitude.

i. Understanding Digital Resilience

Digital resilience refers to our capacity to withstand and bounce back from the stresses associated with digital technology. It is the strength to resist the pull of notifications and the courage to be present without the safety net of a screen. Here, we explore the concept of digital resilience and its importance in maintaining control over our attention and well-being.

ii. The Power of Intentional Disconnection

Disconnection, in this context, is not about rejection but about intentional choice. We discuss strategies for implementing periods of disconnection, such as digital sabbaticals or "tech-free Tuesdays," and the benefits these practices bring. By stepping back from the digital realm, we can gain perspective, recharge, and return to our digital tasks with a renewed sense of purpose and control.

iii. Fostering Mindfulness and Presence

Mindfulness is the art of being present, and presence is an antidote to the fragmentation caused by digital interruptions. Through Analog Anchors that promote mindfulness, such as meditation or simply sitting quietly and observing our surroundings, we reinforce our ability to focus and be fully engaged in the moment.

iv. The Role of Disconnection in Creativity

Creativity often blooms in the space created by disconnection. We examine how periods of being unplugged can foster creative thinking and problem-solving. Analog Anchors like nature walks or doodling can be the catalysts for new ideas, providing the mental breathing room necessary for innovation.

v. Developing a Disconnection Practice

Building resilience through disconnection is a practice, not a one-off endeavor. We provide practical guidance on developing a personal disconnection practice that works within the context of individual lives. This might involve setting boundaries around device use, engaging in regular analog activities, or finding communities that support a less digitally-centered lifestyle.

vi. Evaluating the Impact of Disconnection

Finally, we assess the impact of these practices. How does regular disconnection affect our stress levels, our relationships, and our productivity? By reviewing research and sharing stories of those who have embraced these principles, we offer evidence of the transformative power of building resilience through disconnection.

In this part of the journey, the reader is invited to consider Analog Anchors not just as quaint counterpoints to technology, but as essential tools in building a robust, resilient self—one capable of navigating both the digital and analog worlds with grace and equanimity.

The Joy of Missing Out (JOMO)

In an era where FOMO (Fear of Missing Out) has become a pervasive anxiety, JOMO (Joy of Missing Out) emerges as its philosophical counterpoint. This section is a deep dive into the liberating concept of JOMO—the pleasure of stepping away from the relentless stream of digital information and social demands to enjoy personal time and space.

i. Embracing JOMO

JOMO is the emotional and psychological fulfillment one experiences when making a conscious choice to unplug and find peace in missing out on social events, online interactions, or the latest viral trends. We explore how embracing JOMO can be a transformative experience, allowing for a richer engagement with life's immediate, tangible joys.

ii. Finding Balance in a Connected World

The art of JOMO lies in finding balance. It's about recognizing that we don't have to attend every event, respond to every notification, or keep up with every piece of news. This segment offers guidance on how to strike a harmonious balance between being informed and connected, and preserving time for solitude and reflection.

iii. Celebrating Solitude

JOMO often requires the embrace of solitude, which can be uncomfortable at first. We explore the cultural stigma around solitude and how to overcome it, highlighting the benefits of spending time alone. Solitude can foster introspection, creativity, and a deepened sense of self-awareness, all of which contribute to personal growth.

iv. Cultivating Mindfulness in the Age of Distraction

Mindfulness practices are a gateway to JOMO. This section details how mindfulness can help us savor our experiences and live more fully in the present. By engaging in mindfulness, we're not just opting out of the digital noise; we're also tuning into the richness of the world around us.

v. The Role of Analog Anchors in JOMO

Analog Anchors serve as powerful tools in the pursuit of JOMO. Engaging with the physical world can naturally lead to moments where we're out of the digital loop—and that's okay. We share practical advice on using Analog Anchors to cultivate JOMO and make these non-digital experiences more fulfilling.

vi. Reframing FOMO into JOMO

Transforming FOMO into JOMO is a matter of reframing our mindset. We delve into cognitive strategies to shift from a sense of loss to a sense of gain when we choose to disconnect. It's about valuing quality over quantity, depth over breadth, and presence over ubiquity.

vii. Testimonials and Success Stories

Real-life stories and testimonials from individuals who have embraced JOMO offer inspiration and tangible proof of its benefits. These narratives illustrate the wide array of joys that become available to us when we're willing to occasionally step back from the digital world.

Concluding the section, we propose that JOMO is not just a temporary escape from digital overload but can be a lifelong lifestyle choice. It's a commitment to prioritize personal well-being and meaningful experiences over digital consumption—a choice that, while it may go against the mainstream, promises a richer, more connected life in the truest sense.

Integrating Analog Anchors into Daily Life

As we conclude this chapter on Analog Anchors, we reflect on the delicate balance between the digital and analog realms of our existence. The journey towards integrating Analog Anchors into daily life is both personal and universal—each of us must find our own rhythm and rituals that ground us in the physical world. Here, we offer a blueprint for weaving these anchors into the fabric of daily life, ensuring that we maintain our connection to the tangible, sensory world that sustains us.

i. Creating a Personal Inventory

Begin by taking stock of your daily digital habits and identifying moments where an Analog Anchor could be introduced. This could be as simple as replacing the morning email check with a brief meditation or enjoying a cup of coffee without the accompaniment of a screen.

ii. Small Steps for Significant Change

The transformation doesn't have to be radical; small, incremental changes often lead to sustainable habits. Start with one Analog Anchor and allow it to naturally become a part of your routine before introducing another.

iii. Designing Your Environment

Your environment greatly influences your habits. Design your living and working spaces to encourage Analog Anchoring—keep a book or a sketchpad within easy reach, have a dedicated space for journaling or meditation, and create tech-free zones in your home.

iv. Setting Boundaries with Technology

Boundaries are vital. Designate times of the day or week as digital-free periods. Use these times to engage with your Analog Anchors, whether it's going for a walk, cooking a meal from scratch, or simply sitting and thinking.

v. Rituals Over Routines

Transform your Analog Anchors into rituals, infusing them with intention and meaning. A ritualistic approach turns simple activities into profound practices that nourish your mind and spirit.

vi. Embracing Community and Solitude

Some Analog Anchors are communal—shared meals, group sports, or book clubs—while others are solitary. Value both types of experiences for their unique benefits and incorporate a mix into your life.

vii. The Power of Reflection

Regularly reflect on the impact of these Analog Anchors. Keep a journal to note any changes in your well-being, productivity, and happiness. Adjust your practices as you learn what works best for you.

viii. Sharing the Journey

Share your experiences with friends and family. Discussing the benefits and challenges of integrating Analog Anchors can provide mutual support and inspiration.

Finally, recognize that the integration of Analog Anchors is a life-long practice, not a one-time fix. As digital technologies evolve, so too will the nature and necessity of our Analog Anchors. Commit to remaining adaptable and vigilant, ensuring that as your life changes, your Anchors remain steadfast, keeping you grounded, present, and connected to the very essence of living.

With these strategies in mind, we can cultivate a life that honors both the digital and analog aspects of our existence, harnessing the best of both worlds to live fully, mindfully, and with intention.

4

Strategies for Steady Anchoring

As we navigate the uncharted waters of the digital age, the currents of innovation and the tides of information threaten to sweep us into a relentless cycle of connectivity. Chapter 4, titled "Strategies for Steady Anchoring," is the compass that guides us towards cultivating a balanced existence. In this chapter, we build upon the foundation laid by the concept of Analog Anchors, expanding the narrative from theoretical underpinnings to practical application. These strategies are meticulously designed to empower individuals to plant their feet firmly on the ground, anchoring themselves in the face of the digital gale.

We recognize that the digital realm is not an adversary to be vanquished but a reality to be harmonized with. Our focus is on fostering a symbiotic relationship with our devices and platforms, wherein technology becomes an extension of our will rather than a force that bends us to its own. The strategies herein are crafted with the understanding that intentionality is our rudder in these waters—guiding our digital interactions to be as purposeful as they are powerful, ensuring that our analog experiences remain vivid and vital.

This chapter is a voyage through the practicalities of maintaining equilibrium in the digital deluge. We address the need to curate our digital spaces as diligently as we tend our gardens, pruning the excess and nurturing the necessary. It presents a suite of tools designed to help navigate the fine line between being washed away by digital distractions and leveraging technology to enhance our journey through life.

We will delve into methodologies for auditing and adjusting our digital consumption, ideas for engaging with technology mindfully, and tactics for carving out sacred spaces untouched by the web of connectivity. Here, readers will learn how to reclaim time from the voracious appetite of the digital beast, rekindle the depth of face-to-face human interactions, and establish professional boundaries that protect one's right to disconnect.

"Strategies for Steady Anchoring" is not just a set of guidelines but a manifesto for the intentional life, one where each person's unique values and aspirations dictate their digital engagements. As we turn the pages, we transition from a reactive stance to a proactive one, embracing the tools of our age without becoming tools ourselves. We are the captains of our ships, and with these strategies, we chart a course towards a horizon where our humanity is enhanced, not eclipsed, by the digital sun.

Diagnosis: Assessing Your Digital Habits

i. Self-Audit

Begin by documenting your digital usage over the course of a typical week. Utilize apps that track screen time or maintain a manual log. Be meticulous and honest. The goal is to paint a vivid picture of your digital day-to-day—how often you check your phone, the first thing you do upon waking up, the last screen you see before sleep, and the moments you feel compelled to share online. Once gathered, this data serves as the bedrock for understanding your digital habits.

Techniques for this self-audit might include:

- **Quantitative Tracking:** Utilizing built-in digital wellbeing features on your devices to log screen time, app usage, and notifications.
- **Qualitative Journaling:** Keeping a diary of your emotional responses to digital interactions. Were you seeking connection, entertainment, distraction, or information?
- **Behavioral Observation:** Noting the circumstances under which you engage digitally. Are there patterns or triggers, such as boredom or stress, that prompt your usage?

ii. Priority Matrix

With your digital habits laid bare, the next step is to categorize these behaviors using a Priority Matrix. This matrix will help you discern which digital tools and activities are vital (high priority and high frequency) and which are superfluous (low priority and low frequency).

To create your Priority Matrix, follow these steps:

- **List all digital activities:** From checking emails to scrolling through social media, include even the seemingly trivial.
- **Assign priority levels:** Determine the importance of each activity based on your personal and professional goals. Consider what activities are truly beneficial to your life.
- **Evaluate frequency:** Note how often you engage in each activity. Is the frequency justified by the activity's importance?
- **Create quadrants:** Draw a two-by-two matrix. Label one axis "Importance" and the other "Frequency." Place each activity in one of the four quadrants (High Importance/High Frequency, High Importance/Low Frequency, Low Importance/High Frequency, Low Importance/Low Frequency).

The Priority Matrix allows you to visualize which digital habits warrant maintenance and which present opportunities for reduction or elimination. With this clarity, you can begin to formulate a plan for digital decluttering, consciously choosing which digital waves to ride and which to let pass by

Cultivating Mindfulness: The Art of Intentional Use

i. Digital Mindfulness Practices

Mindfulness in the digital realm involves becoming acutely aware of your online activities and intentions. It's about bringing a sense of purpose to each click and swipe rather than moving through the digital space on autopilot.

Techniques for fostering digital mindfulness may include:

- **Mindful Browsing:** Before opening a browser or app, take a moment to articulate why you are doing it. This pause can help you avoid mindless scrolling.
- **Notification Meditation:** Reflect on each notification you receive. Consider whether it merits immediate attention or if it can wait, thereby reducing the reactive nature of digital interruptions.
- **Single-Tasking:** Engage with one digital task at a time. For example, if you are reading an article online, resist the urge to simultaneously check emails or messages.

ii. Intentional Interactions

Digital platforms are tools, and like any tool, their value lies in how they are used. Intentional interaction is about using these tools deliberately, in ways that are consistent with your values and beneficial to your well-being.

Steps to ensure your interactions are intentional:

- **Alignment with Goals:** Before engaging with any digital content or platform, ask yourself if this interaction moves you closer to your personal or professional goals.
- **Value-Based Consumption:** Favor digital content that enriches your life, whether it's educational, inspiring, or helps you maintain meaningful connections.
- **Scheduled Engagements:** Allocate specific times for digital activities. For example, decide in advance when you will check social media or play online games, and stick to these designated times.

By applying these practices, you create a digital environment where mindfulness is the norm. This approach not only enhances the quality of your digital experiences but also frees up cognitive and emotional space for offline pursuits that provide deeper fulfillment.

Detoxification: Periods of Digital Abstinence

i. Digital Detox Retreats

These are intentional breaks from digital devices, ranging from a few hours to several days or even weeks. The aim is to disconnect from the constant stream of digital information and interactions to allow your mind to reset and recharge. Retreats can be as simple as designating an evening each week where all digital devices are turned off, or as involved as a weekend getaway in nature without any electronics.

Key components of a digital detox retreat could include:

- **Preparation:** Informing friends, family, and colleagues that you will be unavailable digitally during this time to set expectations.
- **Physical Disconnection:** Storing devices in a specific location out of sight to avoid temptation.
- **Replacement Activities:** Engaging in alternative activities that you enjoy or find relaxing, such as reading, crafting, or outdoor sports.

ii. Long-Term Detox Strategies

While short-term retreats can provide temporary relief, developing a long-term strategy for regular digital detoxes can lead to more sustainable benefits. This might mean establishing routines that incorporate regular intervals of disconnection, or even re-evaluating and reducing the role that digital technology plays in your life.

For a sustainable long-term detox approach, consider:

- **Regular Scheduling:** Establishing a routine, such as a "tech-free Tuesday" or a weekend morning without screens, can provide consistent opportunities for disconnection.
- **Tech-Free Zones:** Creating specific areas in your home where digital devices are not allowed, such as the bedroom or dining room, to foster a better digital-life balance.
- **Mindful Consumption:** Developing an ongoing practice of mindful engagement with technology, ensuring that when you do connect, it's deliberate and purposeful.

Both short-term retreats and long-term strategies are about creating space for yourself away from the digital world. This space can lead to increased creativity, a clearer mind, and a greater appreciation for your analog life.

Reclamation: Taking Back Time

i. Time Ownership

This concept revolves around the principle that you should control how your time is spent, rather than letting external demands, especially from digital technology, dictate your schedule. Owning your time requires awareness of how you're currently spending your hours and making conscious decisions to change that where necessary.

To truly own your time, consider:

- **Time Tracking:** Keep a log for a week to see where your time actually goes, especially the minutes eaten up by unplanned digital scrolling.
- **Boundary Setting:** Create clear boundaries for when and how you use digital devices, like no emails after 7 PM or no social media during work hours.

ii. Activity Replacement

The idea here is to replace time spent on less fulfilling digital activities with analog experiences that provide greater fulfillment and joy. By engaging in more meaningful activities, you can enhance the quality of your life.

Strategies for activity replacement might include:

- **Hobby Development:** Investing time in hobbies that don't involve screens, like painting, writing, or playing a musical instrument.
- **Social Reconnection:** Making an effort to spend more time with friends and family in person, or connecting over a phone call rather than through social media or texting.

The reclamation of time isn't just about cutting out digital; it's about re-prioritizing your life to focus on activities that align with your values and enhance your well-being. This deliberate shift can lead to a richer, more controlled experience of your own life.

Technological Triage: Essentialism in the Digital Sphere

i. App Minimalism

This practice involves critically evaluating the apps and digital services in your life, keeping only those that serve essential functions or significantly enhance your well-being. It's about simplifying your digital landscape so that you engage only with technology that adds value to your life.

For app minimalism, consider:

- **App Audits:** Regularly review and uninstall apps that are not essential or that you do not use frequently.
- **Functionality Duplication:** Remove apps that have overlapping functions unless they offer a unique, indispensable benefit.

ii. Notification Management

With this strategy, you curtail the interruption economy by taking control over what alerts deserve your immediate attention. Managing notifications helps maintain focus and reduces the constant pull of your attention to your devices.

To manage notifications effectively:

- *Selective Silence:* Turn off non-essential notifications. Choose only to receive alerts for high-priority items, such as direct messages or calls from family.
- *Scheduled Checks:* Allocate specific times for checking different types of notifications, rather than allowing them to interrupt at will.

By applying technological triage, you actively prioritize your digital tools, creating a more intentional and less cluttered digital environment. This approach aligns your technology use with your core priorities and reduces the digital noise that can disrupt your day-to-day life.

Relationship Rethink: Fostering Real-World Connections

i. Quality over Quantity

This tenet encourages a focus on cultivating deeper, more meaningful relationships with fewer people, rather than maintaining superficial connections with a large number of digital acquaintances. It's about depth and quality of interaction rather than the breadth of your social network.

For fostering quality relationships:

- *Conscious Communication:* Choose more personal and impactful forms of communication, like phone calls or meetups, over text messages or social media likes.
- *Invested Time:* Prioritize spending time with those who are important to you and where mutual support and engagement are strong.

ii. Community Building

This involves a deliberate effort to create and nurture physical communities that offer support, shared experiences, and a sense of belonging. Local community engagement can provide a counterbalance to the often dispersed and virtual networks we participate in online.

Strategies for community building:

- *Local Events:* Attend or organize local meetups, workshops, or community service events that align with your interests.
- *Neighborhood Initiatives:* Engage in neighborhood groups or activities that foster a sense of local camaraderie and support.

By rethinking our approach to relationships in this way, we can foster a more supportive and interconnected environment that enhances our well-being and gives us a tangible sense of belonging in an increasingly digital world.

Professional Boundaries: Work in the Age of Constant Connectivity

i. Email Etiquette

As the cornerstone of professional communication, email can also be a source of constant distraction. Implementing clear boundaries around email can mitigate this.

Guidelines for better email etiquette:

- *Scheduled Checks:* Designate specific times for checking and responding to emails rather than reacting to each notification.
- *Clear Expectations:* Communicate with colleagues and clients about your email response times, reducing the pressure for immediate replies.

ii. Task Segmentation

In a digital environment that promotes multitasking, it's crucial to establish boundaries for more efficient and focused work.

Ways to implement task segmentation:

- *Time Blocking:* Allocate specific blocks of time to different tasks or projects, avoiding the inefficiency of frequent switching.
- *Technology Zones:* Create physical or virtual spaces dedicated to specific types of work, helping to minimize cross-task interference.

Establishing professional boundaries like these helps maintain a work-life balance, protect personal time, and enhance productivity by reducing the cognitive load that comes with the digital sprawl of modern work life.

Education and Play: Rediscovering Non-Digital Learning and Leisure

i. Educational Anchors

This involves a recommitment to analog educational materials and environments that foster deep learning and retention.

Strategies include:

- *Hands-On Learning:* Emphasizing tactile, hands-on activities that engage different learning styles and promote memory retention.
- *Printed Materials:* Using books, printed worksheets, and other physical materials to reduce screen time and improve focus during learning sessions.

ii. Play Unplugged

Encourages a break from screens to engage in physical play, which is crucial for cognitive and physical development in children and stress relief in adults.

Approaches to encourage unplugged play:

- *Structured Unplugged Time:* Setting aside specific times when electronic devices are turned off, creating space for other activities.
- *Outdoor Activities:* Promoting outdoor play, which provides opportunities for exercise, imagination, and interaction with the natural world.

By incorporating educational anchors and unplugged play into our routines, we can create a balanced lifestyle that values both the digital and analog aspects of learning and leisure, fostering a holistic development that is essential in the digital age.

Crafting and Creating: The Analog Makerspace

This section is about embracing the do-it-yourself ethos and finding joy in the creative process that is often untapped by digital distractions.

i. DIY Culture

It's about reconnecting with the process of making and doing things ourselves, using skills that require us to step away from the screen and engage with the physical world.

Key points include:

- *Skill Development:* Encouraging the learning of new hands-on skills, from woodworking to sewing, that offer a sense of accomplishment and tangible results.
- *Project-Based Learning:* Promoting project-based activities that result in a physical product, reinforcing the value of patience and persistence.

ii. Creative Flow

Focuses on the psychological concept of 'flow', a state of immersion in a task that is both challenging and rewarding.

Methods to foster creative flow:

- *Dedicated Creative Spaces:* Establishing physical spaces at home or in the community dedicated to crafting and creating, free from digital interruptions.
- *Time Management for Creativity:* Allocating uninterrupted time for engaging in creative pursuits, allowing for deeper concentration and satisfaction from the act of creation.

Through crafting and creating in analog spaces, we not only cultivate personal skills and satisfaction but also build communities centered around shared interests and the collective experience of making.

A Balanced Digital-Analog Life

In the conclusion of our journey through establishing Analog Anchors and managing the digital deluge, we reflect on the importance of setting personal boundaries and policies for technology use.

Personal Policies: This involves creating and adhering to a personal code of conduct regarding digital consumption. It could include specific times of day for checking emails, a commitment to disconnect from all digital devices during meals, or weekend tech breaks. These policies aren't about imposing restrictions but rather about designing a life that allows for the mindful use of technology.

Evolving with Technology: As technology evolves, so too should our strategies for integrating it into our lives. Staying anchored doesn't mean resisting change; it means having a clear sense of what keeps you grounded and adjusting your sails as the digital winds shift. This could mean adopting new tools that align with your values or discarding old habits that no longer serve you.

This balanced approach isn't a one-time fix but a continuous process of calibration, ensuring that our digital interactions enhance rather than dictate the quality of our lives. By maintaining this equilibrium, we can enjoy the benefits of technology while preserving the richness of a life deeply rooted in the analog world. The conclusion leaves readers with a sense of empowerment and the tools to curate a life that resonates with their deepest intentions, values, and joys.

This chapter is about more than temporary fixes or one-off experiments; it's about setting in place a lifelong practice of balanced tech use. By systematically implementing these strategies, readers can create a personal ecosystem where technology serves as a tool for enhancing life, not detracting from it.

5

Redefining Productivity

This chapter challenges the traditional digital-centric view of efficiency and output. In the wake of our discussions on Analog Anchors, we turn our attention to how we can redefine productivity in a manner that honors both our human need for deep work and the inevitable integration of technology in our lives. This chapter seeks to dispel the myth that constant connectivity equates to higher productivity, advocating instead for a more nuanced understanding that values quality and meaning in our professional and personal endeavors.

Dissecting the Myth of Digital Efficiency

i. The Digital Tool Paradox

The Digital Tool Paradox explores the complex and often counterintuitive relationship between the proliferation of digital tools and apps and the actual productivity of individuals and organizations. It challenges the prevalent notion that more digital resources invariably lead to increased efficiency and effectiveness.

Origins of the Productivity Paradox: The belief in digital tools as unequivocal enhancers of productivity has roots in the early days of the computer age. Initially, the introduction of computers and software in the workplace led to significant leaps in efficiency and output, creating an enduring expectation that more technology equates to better productivity.

The Allure of Multitasking: This misconception was further bolstered by the idea of digital multitasking. With the advent of smartphones and multiple apps, the ability to do several tasks simultaneously was initially seen as a productivity boon. However, subsequent research has shown that multitasking can actually lead to decreased efficiency and more errors.

The App Overload Phenomenon: As the market became inundated with an app for everything, the paradox deepened. The sheer number of digital tools available can lead to cognitive overload, decision fatigue, and a cluttered digital environment where finding and using the right tool becomes a task in itself.

The Illusion of Busy-ness: The constant stream of notifications and the need to stay 'connected' can create an illusion of busy-ness and productivity, where being constantly engaged with digital tools is misconstrued as being productive.

The Quality vs. Quantity Misconception: There's a prevalent misunderstanding that more output, facilitated by digital tools, necessarily means better outcomes. This overlooks the importance of the quality of work, creative thought, and strategic planning, which can be hindered by excessive reliance on digital tools.

Diminishing Returns of Hyper-Connectivity: The paradox also lies in the diminishing returns of being hyper-connected. While digital tools offer the ability to stay constantly in touch and share information rapidly, this can lead to burnout and decreased job satisfaction, impacting overall productivity.

The Rise of Digital Minimalism: In response, there's a growing movement towards digital minimalism. This philosophy advocates for the thoughtful use of digital tools, focusing on quality over quantity and encouraging individuals to consciously choose their digital engagements to enhance productivity and personal well-being.

Cultural and Corporate Shifts: Corporations and individuals are increasingly recognizing the need for a cultural shift in how digital tools are perceived and used. There's a move towards policies that encourage focused work periods without digital interruption, promoting a balanced approach to technology use.

Redefining Productivity: The conversation is shifting from equating productivity with constant activity and output to a more holistic view that values creativity, innovation, mental health, and strategic thinking.

The Digital Tool Paradox urges a reexamination of our relationship with digital tools. It advocates for a more mindful and intentional approach to technology, recognizing that while digital tools have the potential to enhance productivity, their unbridled use can have the opposite effect. The key lies in finding a balance that leverages technology effectively without becoming subservient to it.

The Multitasking Mirage: Investigating the impact of digital multitasking on our work quality and output. This subsection will delve into cognitive science to understand how our brains respond to juggling multiple tasks and the long-term repercussions on both productivity and mental health.

The Productivity Plateau: Analyzing how the initial productivity gains from digital tools eventually plateau and can lead to a decrease in overall efficiency. Through case studies and research, this part will explore the thresholds of digital utility and the point at which additional tools become counterproductive.

Digital Saturation and Cognitive Load: Discussing how an overabundance of digital tools can lead to cognitive overload, hindering our ability to think creatively and solve complex problems effectively. Strategies will be provided to identify and reduce unnecessary digital clutter.

ii. Deep Work in a Shallow World

Embracing Newport's Philosophy: Diving into the core principles of Cal Newport's concept of 'Deep Work'—the ability to focus without distraction on cognitively demanding tasks. This subsection will explain how to apply these principles to various professional environments and personal endeavors.

Creating Sanctuaries of Concentration: Detailing how to design and maintain physical and digital environments that encourage deep work. This will include discussions on managing space, time, and technology to minimize distractions.

The Deep Work Ritual: Introducing the idea of structured routines and rituals to enter a state of deep work. Profiles of successful individuals who have harnessed the power of deep work through consistent habits will illustrate this approach.

Digital Minimalism for Maximum Focus: Applying the tenets of digital minimalism to clear the path for deep work. Techniques for reducing digital noise and strategically using technology will be presented to help readers focus on demanding tasks.

Strategies for Sustaining Deep Work: Offering practical tips and strategies to sustain periods of deep concentration over longer timescales, including advice on managing energy levels, scheduling deep work sessions, and the importance of taking breaks aligned with the body's natural rhythms.

Overcoming Resistance to Deep Work: Addressing common psychological barriers to engaging in deep work, such as the allure of social media and instant gratification, and providing methods to overcome these challenges through habit formation and self-discipline.

iii. The Power of Unplugging

Recharging Through Disconnection: This section will highlight the importance of taking breaks from digital devices to recharge one's mental batteries. The reader will understand how non-digital periods can increase overall productivity by allowing for mental rest and recovery.

Empirical Evidence of Unplugging: We'll delve into research studies and statistical data that demonstrate the benefits of regular digital detoxes. This evidence will show correlations between disconnection and improvements in concentration, problem-solving abilities, and creativity.

Case Studies of Successful Unpluggers: Through a series of anecdotes and case studies, the experiences of individuals and companies that have instituted policies of regular unplugging will be examined, showcasing the positive impact on work output and employee well-being.

Scheduled Disconnection for Optimal Output: Offering a blueprint for integrating scheduled disconnections into one's personal and professional life. This will include guidance on how to balance connectivity with strategic offline intervals to enhance productivity.

Mindfulness and Meditation as Unplugging Practices: Discussion on the use of mindfulness techniques and meditation as tools to unplug effectively. These practices can provide similar cognitive benefits as digital disconnection and can be used in tandem with or as a supplement to time away from screens.

Long-Term Productivity through Short-Term Unplugging: Concluding with an examination of how regular intervals of disconnection contribute to long-term productivity gains. The reader will learn how to incorporate unplugging into a lifestyle choice, supporting a sustainable and healthy work-life balance.

iv. Quality Over Quantity: Metrics That Matter

Redefining Productivity: This segment explores a paradigm shift from traditional productivity metrics, which often prioritize busyness, to modern metrics that focus on the outcomes and impact of work. Readers will learn about the importance of measuring the right things and how that can change their view of what being productive actually means.

Outcome-Based Productivity: We delve into strategies for setting goals and benchmarks that are oriented towards the quality of outcomes rather than the quantity of tasks completed. This includes examining how to define success in ways that align with personal and organizational values.

Impactful Work versus Busy Work: Distinguishing between work that genuinely moves projects forward and tasks that simply take up time. We will discuss how to identify high-leverage activities that have a substantial effect on overall progress and satisfaction.

Setting and Measuring Value-Driven Metrics: This section will provide guidance on how to establish and track metrics that matter to you or your organization. It will include examples of value-driven metrics across various domains and how these can be tied to broader goals and objectives.

Tools for Tracking Quality Metrics: An overview of tools and systems that can help monitor and report on productivity metrics focused on quality. We will examine digital and analog tools that are best suited for tracking different types of metrics.

Case Studies of Value-Centric Workflows: Real-world examples of individuals and businesses that have successfully implemented outcome-focused productivity measures will be showcased. Lessons learned from these case studies will offer insights into best practices and potential pitfalls.

Creating a Culture of Quality: Final thoughts on how to foster an environment, whether at work or at home, that celebrates high-quality outcomes. This will include tips for encouraging oneself and others to focus on work that truly matters, thus enhancing both productivity and fulfillment.

v. Rhythms of Rest: The Role of Downtime

Understanding Rest's Vital Function: This section initiates a conversation on the often-underestimated value of rest in the productivity equation. Readers are introduced to the science behind rest and how it directly impacts cognitive functions, creativity, and overall job performance.

Rest as a Strategic Asset: We explore the idea of rest not as a reward for hard work but as a critical strategy for peak performance. The discussion will revolve around how planned rest can lead to sustained productivity and a healthier work-life balance.

Sleep Science and Productivity: Delving into the relationship between sleep quality and productivity, this part of the chapter outlines sleep patterns, stages, and hygiene. It also addresses the negative impacts of sleep deficit and offers guidelines for improving sleep.

Designing Effective Breaks: Insights into the art of scheduling breaks to maximize recovery and minimize fatigue. Techniques such as the Pomodoro Technique, mindfulness breaks, and movement breaks are considered, with advice on how to personalize these for individual needs.

Leisure and Unstructured Time: The importance of leisure and hobbies is emphasized, discussing how activities unrelated to work can contribute to problem-solving abilities and creative thinking. The chapter examines how engaging in play and pursuits outside of work can actually enhance professional growth.

Cultivating a Restful Mindset: This segment focuses on psychological approaches to rest, such as the practice of mindfulness and meditation, and their role in disconnecting from work-related stressors to recharge the mind.

Incorporating Downtime into Daily Routines: Practical steps for integrating rest into everyday life, including establishing routines that make rest a non-negotiable part of the day, much like important meetings or project deadlines.

Case Studies and Success Stories: To wrap up the chapter, readers are presented with examples of successful individuals and companies that attribute part of their success to integrating rhythms of rest into their operational models, offering inspiration and concrete evidence of the principles discussed.

vi. Analog Tools for Modern Times

The Tangible Touch: This section reintroduces the tactile experience of analog tools and discusses their psychological benefits. We explore why the act of writing or drawing on physical media can anchor thoughts more effectively than typing on a digital device.

Paper Planners in the Digital Age: An in-depth look at the enduring appeal of paper planners. Despite the ubiquity of digital calendars and apps, this part explains why many still prefer the old-school method of jotting down their schedules, highlighting the planner's role in mindfulness and intentionality.

Whiteboards: Visual Thinking Spaces: Here, we examine how whiteboards serve as a canvas for mapping out ideas and concepts in a collaborative space. The utility of whiteboards in brainstorming sessions, project planning, and the fluid nature of idea development in a group setting is discussed.

Notebooks: The Unassuming Idea Vaults: The value of keeping a personal notebook is celebrated, with a nod to historical figures who used notebooks to capture fleeting thoughts, musings, and breakthroughs. We discuss how notebooks can act as a private dialogue with oneself, fostering insight and creativity.

Index Cards: Organizing Thoughts and Tasks: Index cards, often overlooked, are presented as a powerful method for organizing thoughts, tasks, and projects. We delve into systems like the Zettelkasten method that leverage these cards for complex information management and knowledge development.

The Role of Analog in Time Management: This section links analog methods to effective time management, exploring how the physical act of writing down tasks and crossing them off can lead to a more disciplined and focused approach to managing one's time.

Combining Analog and Digital: We discuss strategies for integrating analog tools into digital workflows, such as using scanning apps to digitize written notes or syncing written agendas with digital calendars, thus marrying the best of both worlds.

Case Studies: Analog Tools in High-Tech Environments: Finally, the chapter presents case studies from various fields where analog tools have been successfully integrated into modern, high-tech environments, demonstrating how they enhance productivity, creativity, and team cohesion.

vii. Streamlining Digital Workflows

Simplicity in Structure: This section addresses the importance of establishing simple, intuitive structures within digital environments. It discusses methods for organizing files, emails, and digital documents to reduce clutter and enhance accessibility.

Automation Advantage: Here, we delve into the benefits of automating repetitive tasks. From email filters to project management tools, we explore how setting up the right automation can free up mental space and time.

Digital Decluttering: Like tidying a physical space, this part emphasizes the need for regular digital clean-ups. We provide actionable advice for auditing and purging unnecessary digital content, which can lead to a more streamlined and efficient workflow.

App Synergy: The focus here is on selecting digital tools that work well together, creating an ecosystem where data can flow smoothly from one application to another, thereby increasing efficiency and reducing friction.

Task Batching: This section introduces the concept of task batching in the digital realm, explaining how grouping similar tasks together can minimize context switching and promote a more focused approach to work.

The One-Touch Principle: Based on the concept of handling things only once, we discuss how applying the one-touch principle to digital tasks (such as email management) can reduce backlog and decision fatigue.

Prioritizing with Digital Tools: We explore how digital tools can aid in prioritization, using features like color-coding, tagging, and prioritization matrices to keep the most important tasks visible and top-of-mind.

Templates and Checklists: The creation and use of digital templates and checklists are presented as a way to standardize processes and ensure consistency, which in turn can speed up workflows and ensure quality control.

Cutting Through the Noise: Tips for managing and reducing digital interruptions, such as notifications and alerts, are provided. This part of the chapter encourages readers to set boundaries that allow them to work with greater focus.

Data Management: Lastly, we tackle the issue of data management, providing insights into organizing and securing data in a way that protects against loss and makes retrieval straightforward and fast.

viii. Setting Boundaries for Tech and Task

Defining Digital Limits: This section emphasizes the importance of establishing specific time frames for using digital devices and platforms. It guides the reader through the process of creating a digital schedule that aligns with productivity goals and personal well-being.

Selective Tech Usage: Here, the focus is on the conscious selection of technology for particular tasks, recommending the use of digital tools only when they provide a clear advantage over analog alternatives.

Creating Tech-Free Zones: This part advocates for the designation of certain areas in the home or office as tech-free zones, places where digital devices are not allowed, to encourage uninterrupted work or rest.

Permission to Disconnect: The chapter discusses the psychological and practical aspects of giving oneself permission to disconnect from technology, especially outside of working hours or during personal time.

Task-Specific Technology: We explore the concept of using technology tailored to specific tasks to prevent the temptation of multitasking and to maintain focus on the task at hand.

Technology Curfews: Implementing technology curfews is presented as a strategy to reduce the negative impacts of blue light on sleep patterns and to help establish a healthy work-life balance.

Mindful Notifications: This section is about customizing notifications to ensure that only the most important alerts are received, thus reducing the constant demand on one's attention and the associated stress.

Managing Digital Overwhelm: We offer strategies for coping with and reducing the sense of overwhelm that can come from excessive digital communication and information overload.

Assertive Communication: Techniques for assertively communicating one's digital boundaries to friends, family, and colleagues are provided, along with ways to reinforce these boundaries without causing offense.

Psychological Strategies: The chapter concludes with psychological strategies to deal with the urge to check digital devices constantly, including habit-reversal training and cognitive-behavioral approaches that help to strengthen self-discipline and maintain set boundaries.

ix. Mindfulness and Presence: The Ultimate Productivity Tools

Cultivating Mindful Practices: This section introduces various mindfulness practices that can be integrated into daily routines to enhance concentration and presence, such as meditation, focused breathing exercises, and mindful walking.

Presence in Task Management: We discuss how being fully present during task execution can lead to higher quality work, offering strategies for minimizing distractions and fostering a state of flow.

Mindfulness Training for Focus: Here, readers will find methods for training the mind to stay present and resist the pull of multitasking, including exercises that build the mental muscle needed for sustained attention.

The Intersection of Mindfulness and Technology: This part explores how to use technology in a way that supports rather than undermines mindfulness, such as apps for guided meditation or tools that limit digital interruptions.

Evaluating Productivity Through Mindfulness: We examine how a mindful approach to work can redefine productivity, moving away from quantity and towards a focus on the quality and purposefulness of output.

Mindfulness-Based Stress Reduction (MBSR): This section delves into the MBSR program and how its principles can be applied to reduce work-related stress and enhance overall productivity.

The Ripple Effect of Presence: The chapter looks at how cultivating presence can positively impact not just individual productivity but also improve team dynamics and communication.

Mindful Leadership: Readers will learn about the concept of mindful leadership, where leaders leverage presence and mindfulness to create more responsive and adaptive teams and organizations.

Balancing Productivity and Well-being: The concluding part emphasizes how mindfulness can balance the drive for productivity with the need for personal well-being, leading to sustainable work habits and a more fulfilling life.

Implementing a Mindfulness Routine: Practical guidance is provided on how to establish a consistent mindfulness routine, tailored to individual lifestyles, to reap the benefits of increased presence in both personal and professional spheres.

x. Creating a Productivity Plan That Works for You

Assessment of Individual Work Styles: This section encourages readers to reflect on their unique work preferences and requirements. It includes self-assessment tools to help identify when, where, and how one is most productive.

The Personal Productivity Blueprint: Step-by-step guidance on creating a personalized productivity plan. This blueprint factors in personal goals, strengths, weaknesses, and lifestyle needs.

Balancing Flexibility and Structure: We explore how to balance the need for a structured schedule with the flexibility to adapt to life's unpredictabilities, ensuring that the productivity plan is both effective and realistic.

Integration of Digital and Analog Tools: This part provides advice on how to integrate digital and analog tools seamlessly into one's productivity strategy, emphasizing the use of technology as a facilitator rather than a distractor.

Setting Realistic Goals and Milestones: Techniques for setting achievable goals that motivate rather than overwhelm, including the SMART (Specific, Measurable, Achievable, Relevant, Time-bound) criteria for goal-setting.

Adaptability and Review Cycles: Discussing the importance of regularly reviewing and adjusting the productivity plan to reflect personal growth and changes in circumstances.

The Role of Habit Formation: Tips for developing productivity-boosting habits that stick, including the science of habit formation and how to harness it to reinforce one's productivity plan.

Leveraging Peak Hours: Understanding one's circadian rhythms and learning to schedule the most demanding tasks for times of peak energy.

Overcoming Procrastination and Analysis Paralysis: Strategies for tackling procrastination and decision-making difficulties that can hinder productivity.

Continual Learning and Growth: Emphasizing the importance of life-long learning and personal development as components of productivity, and how to incorporate them into a daily and weekly routine.

Success Measurement: Defining what success looks like on a personal level, beyond traditional productivity metrics, to ensure the plan aligns with one's definition of fulfillment and satisfaction.

Action Steps for Implementation: The chapter concludes with actionable steps to take immediate action on creating and implementing a personalized productivity plan, including templates and resources to get started.

The journey through redefining productivity culminates in a reflective conclusion that underscores the importance of intentionality in how we approach our tasks, time, and energy. It is here that we take a step back to contemplate the broader implications of our productivity pursuits:

- *Beyond Efficiency:* This section encourages readers to look past mere efficiency — the speed and ease with which tasks are completed — and to consider the effectiveness and meaningfulness of their work. It's a call to align tasks with one's core values and life's mission.
- *The Value of Fulfillment:* We discuss how a personal productivity philosophy isn't just about output, but also about the satisfaction and joy derived from one's work. It argues for a definition of productivity that is as much about personal fulfillment as it is about societal contribution.
- *Crafting a Life of Purpose:* Here, readers are prompted to think of productivity not as an end in itself but as a means to a more purposeful life. It's about ensuring that the way we use our time is contributing to a larger picture of who we want to be and the life we want to lead.

- *Embracing a Holistic View:* The conclusion posits that true productivity encompasses all aspects of life — from career and creativity to relationships and personal well-being. It suggests that a balanced approach to productivity is key to overall life satisfaction.
- *The Call for Mindful Productivity:* We emphasize the need for mindfulness in our daily routines, ensuring that we remain aware and present in our activities, and that we're not just going through the motions in a quest for efficiency.
- *Resilience Through Reflection:* The chapter ends by highlighting the importance of regular reflection on our productivity practices. It encourages readers to be resilient in the face of the inevitable productivity ebbs and flows and to view each day as an opportunity to practice intentionality in their actions.

The final message is one of empowerment: with the right approach, tools, and mindset, each individual can redefine productivity in a way that brings harmony between their digital and analog lives, leading to a richer, more intentional existence.

6

The Richness of Analog Experiences

Amidst the hum of digital advancement, our sensory landscape often narrows to the glow of screens, leaving a void where richer, more textured experiences once lay. Chapter 6, titled "The Richness of Analog Experiences," invites readers to rediscover the depth and breadth of a life infused with tactile, sensory-rich activities. This journey reacquaints us with the nuances that tactile engagement brings to our well-being, creativity, and sense of connection. As we navigate through the vast offerings of analog endeavors—from the intimate act of crafting a hand-written note to the labor of love that goes into building a piece of furniture by hand—we stitch a tapestry of real-world experiences that nourish our being far beyond the digital ether. Engaging with the material world in these ways fosters a profound sense of presence, grounding us in the here and now and reminding us of the multifaceted nature of human experience. This chapter is an ode to the beauty of the palpable, an exploration of how analog activities can enrich our lives in an age where the digital often dominates.

i. The Joy of Tactile Activities

Gardening with Hands-On Love: This passage delves into the gritty delight and restorative power of gardening, where hands meet soil, seeds, and life blooms. It illustrates the deep sense of connection and tranquility that comes from nurturing growth with one's own hands. The section shares insights into the therapeutic benefits of gardening, how it can reduce stress, enhance mood, and foster an intimate bond with the cycles of nature.

The Art of Handicrafts: This segment explores the tactile joy and fulfillment found in handicrafts such as knitting, woodworking, and painting. It discusses how these activities engage fine motor skills, concentration, and creativity, offering a unique form of satisfaction that comes from creating something tangible. Through personal anecdotes and research, the text underscores how handicrafts can be a source of pride and personal expression, as well as a counterbalance to the ephemeral nature of digital interactions.

ii. Embracing the Analog in Everyday Life

Analog Living Spaces: This section champions the concept of crafting living environments that inspire and facilitate analog engagements. It offers guidance on how to thoughtfully design our personal spaces to minimize digital distractions and maximize opportunities for physical interaction and presence. This could involve creating dedicated reading nooks, music corners, or art stations that invite creativity and relaxation without the need for electronic devices.

Culinary Adventures Offline: The text ventures into the kitchen, where the analog magic of cooking and baking unfolds. It paints a vivid picture of the joys found in the tactile process of preparing food—the feel of dough beneath fingers, the sizzle of spices hitting the pan, and the aroma of fresh ingredients melding together. It also emphasizes the communal joy and deeper connection that comes from sharing a meal with others, an experience often diminished by digital interferences.

Tips for creating engaging, screen-free culinary experiences are shared, encouraging readers to rediscover the simple pleasure of nourishing body and soul in the company of loved ones.

iii. Analog Learning and Knowledge

Books as Sacred Spaces: This passage extolls the unique tactile and sensory experiences that physical books provide. It discusses how the act of turning pages, feeling the paper's texture, and the very weight of a book create an intimate and focused space for reading and reflection. In an era of digital screens, this section reveres the book as an artifact that holds not just words but a physical presence in our lives, often becoming a cherished vessel of knowledge and memory.

Learning by Doing: The narrative moves to the educational power of hands-on learning, an approach that reinforces knowledge through direct physical experience. By highlighting examples such as building a model, performing a science experiment, or repairing a mechanical device, this section presents the argument that engaging the body alongside the mind promotes deeper understanding and retention of information. It argues that experiential learning in an analog context can foster critical thinking, problem-solving skills, and a tangible sense of achievement that abstract digital simulations often fail to replicate.

iv. Social Interactions in the Real World

Conversations Without Clicks: In this section, the focus shifts to the irreplaceable value of face-to-face conversations. It delves into the nuances of physical presence — the unspoken language of body gestures, the emotional resonance of voice tones, and the genuine connection that eye contact can foster. This part underscores the limitations of digital communication, where clicks and screens act as mediators, and advocates for carving out time and spaces for in-person interactions that foster deeper understanding and bonds.

Community Involvement: The narrative extends into the broader tapestry of community life, emphasizing the benefits of active participation in local events, volunteering, and civic activities. It suggests that involvement in one's community provides a sense of belonging and contributes to the social fabric in a way that online networks cannot. It also highlights how investing in personal relationships within one's physical surroundings can lead to a more fulfilling and grounded life. This section inspires readers to step out of the virtual sphere and immerse themselves in the enriching experiences of collective, real-world endeavors.

v. Leisure Unplugged

The Great Outdoors: Venturing beyond the digital landscape, this part of the chapter champions the rejuvenating power of nature. It encourages readers to embrace outdoor pursuits such as hiking, cycling, and kayaking, highlighting the physical and mental health benefits of such activities. It details how immersing oneself in the natural environment can lead to a disconnection from the digital world, providing a serene space to recharge and reconnect with the earth's rhythms. This section includes tips on how to incorporate outdoor activities into one's routine, emphasizing that even a brief walk in a park can be a potent antidote to digital fatigue.

Board Games and Brain Health: Shifting the focus indoors, this segment explores the resurgence of board games and puzzles as a means of analog entertainment. It articulates the ways in which these activities not only forge social bonds and family connections but also offer significant cognitive benefits. By engaging in strategic play and problem-solving, individuals can enhance their memory, critical thinking skills, and mental agility. This section presents a compelling case for board games as tools for brain health, providing a communal and intellectually stimulating alternative to screen-based leisure. It invites readers to rediscover the joy of gathering around a game, fostering camaraderie and laughter in a shared physical space.

vi. The Creative Process Unbound

Music to One's Ears: This section resonates with the vibrations of music in its most organic form. It underscores the unparalleled experience of creating and partaking in live music, from the strum of a guitar to the harmonies of a choir. Music, in its acoustic essence, offers a respite from the digitized versions that fill our playlists. The chapter conveys the visceral impact of live performance and the intimate connection it fosters among musicians and audiences alike. It provides insights into how engaging with music—whether learning an instrument or attending live performances—can elevate mood, improve cognitive functions, and create a sense of community.

Dance and Movement: Here, the text moves to the rhythm of dance, elucidating its role as a primal form of expression and communication. Dance is presented not just as an art form but as a medium of storytelling and emotional release that predates verbal language. It explores how dance, across its various genres, connects us to our own bodies and to others around us. By encouraging readers to partake in dance, whether in a class, a social setting, or even alone in their living room, the chapter promotes the idea that movement is a powerful tool for physical health and psychological well-being. It paints a picture of dance as an analog activity that can invigorate the spirit, enhance creativity, and forge social bonds in a way that digital interactions often cannot replicate.

vii. Rediscovering Sensory Richness

Expanding Sensory Horizons: This section ventures into the landscape beyond the visual dominance of digital screens, highlighting how analog experiences can fully engage our neglected senses. It discusses the importance of touch in connecting us to our environment, the nuances of taste that remind us of the complexity of our world, the evocative power of scents that can transport us across time, the layers of sound that provide a backdrop to our lives, and the spectrum of sight beyond the pixelated light.

A Symphony of Sensations: Delving into the enriching world of multi-sensory experiences, this part celebrates the intricate dance of sensations we encounter through analog activities. It paints a picture of how non-digital pursuits like cooking, gardening, or playing an instrument can create a harmonious symphony of sensations that resonate with our intrinsic human need for diverse sensory input. This section aims to illustrate the depth and dimension added to our daily lives when we step out of the digital frame and immerse ourselves in the sensory concert of the analog world.

viii. Valuing Presence in the Analog World

As we reach the end of our journey through "The Richness of Analog Experiences," we pause to appreciate the profound essence of presence that is the heart of the analog realm. This chapter culminates in a powerful affirmation of the depth and authenticity that tactile and sensory-rich activities infuse into our lives.

The narrative highlights the contrast between the fleeting, ephemeral nature of digital interactions and the enduring, immersive quality of analog engagements. It emphasizes that while the digital world offers breadth, it is through analog experiences that we find depth. These experiences, from the feel of paper grain beneath our fingertips to the warmth of shared laughter in a room, anchor us firmly in the here and now.

The conclusion calls for a mindful embrace of the physical world, urging us to cherish the simple pleasures that abound when we step away from screens. It is a call to not only exist but to live fully in each moment. By valuing presence, we cultivate a life not just of productivity and efficiency but one of meaning and fulfillment.

In closing, the chapter extends an invitation to readers to see analog experiences not as outdated relics of the past, but as timeless treasures that enrich our existence. It is a gentle prompt to weave these experiences into the fabric of our daily routines, ensuring that our days are marked not by the number of digital notifications we receive, but by the quality of presence we bring to our experiences and interactions.

Ultimately, "The Richness of Analog Experiences" doesn't just encourage us to engage with the world beyond our screens; it inspires us to reconnect with the essence of what it means to be human.

7

Technology, Not Tyranny

In the penultimate chapter of our exploration, we confront the challenge of reclaiming authority over our digital lives. "Technology, Not Tyranny" invites readers to reassess their relationship with digital tools, advocating for a paradigm shift from subjugation to symbiosis. This chapter isn't about discarding our devices but about reframing their role in our lives from that of tyrants to tools, from sources of constant distraction to facilitators of our aspirations.

Through careful examination and mindful practice, we explore how to transform our interactions with technology to enhance, rather than diminish, our human experience. We delve into strategies for using tech tools mindfully, ensuring they serve us rather than ensnare us. This chapter empowers readers to navigate the digital landscape with intention and discernment, embracing technology as a means to enrich our lives rather than a force that detracts from them.

i. Reevaluating Our Digital Tools

Inventory and Introspection: Assessing our digital toolbox to understand our current usage patterns.

In this section, we guide readers through a comprehensive self-assessment to map out their digital landscape. It's a deep dive into the apps, platforms, and devices that populate our daily lives. This inventory goes beyond mere listing; it prompts reflection on the frequency, duration, and quality of interactions with each digital tool. We explore the nuances of our digital routines, distinguishing between tools that add genuine value and those that serve as mere distractions or even detractors from our well-being. This inventory is the bedrock for informed decision-making about which technologies deserve a place in our personal or professional spheres.

Purpose Over Habit: Identifying purpose-driven use of technology versus habitual scrolling and consumption.

Once we have mapped out our digital use, the next step is to scrutinize the intent behind it. Here, we question the 'why' at the heart of our interaction with each tool. Is our use intentional and purposeful, aligning with our goals and values, or is it a reflexive response to boredom, anxiety, or habit? We examine how habitual use of technology can create an illusion of productivity and connectedness, while in reality, it often leads to a fragmented focus and a sense of disconnection from our surroundings and inner selves.

We offer strategies to break the cycle of mindless engagement, such as setting specific goals for technology use, scheduling 'tech-free' times, and consciously choosing analog alternatives. By shifting our approach from passive consumption to active, purpose-driven use, we can transform our digital tools from masters to servants, from sources of compulsion to conduits for enrichment and genuine connectivity. This section arms readers with the tools to cultivate a mindful and intentional digital life, one where technology is wielded with deliberation and purpose.

ii. Mindful Technology Use

Conscious Clicking: Developing habits of intentional online behavior and interaction.

In this focused discourse, we emphasize the power of deliberate action in the digital realm. "Conscious Clicking" is a call to transform our digital reflexes into thoughtful choices. We delve into the psychological underpinnings of impulsive online behaviors and provide practical techniques for cultivating digital mindfulness. Readers are encouraged to pause before they click, reflecting on the purpose and potential impact of their online interactions. This section includes exercises to enhance self-awareness and self-regulation, empowering readers to align their digital behaviors with their most authentic selves.

Mindful Media Consumption: Selecting digital content that aligns with personal growth and well-being.

With an overwhelming barrage of digital content available at our fingertips, "Mindful Media Consumption" is about curating our digital diet as carefully as we would our nutrition. It encourages readers to become discerning consumers of media, choosing content that nourishes the mind and soul rather than that which depletes or distracts. This part of the chapter not only advocates for quality over quantity but also introduces methods for implementing a media consumption plan that supports personal aspirations, mental health, and overall life satisfaction. We explore how to set filters, use technology to limit exposure to negative content, and engage with platforms that truly add value to our lives. This section is about reclaiming the agency over our digital consumption habits and reshaping them to serve our highest goals and ideals.

iii. Digital Spaces as Complements, Not Replacements

Enhancing Reality: Using digital platforms to enhance real-life experiences, not replace them.

This sub-chapter explores how we can leverage digital spaces to augment rather than supplant our real-world experiences. It advocates for a model where technology acts as a backstage assistant, setting the stage for richer, more engaging real-life encounters. We will explore case studies and strategies on how digital tools can facilitate deeper connections, learning, and exploration in the physical world. From augmenting travel experiences with augmented reality to using social media as a means to enhance rather than detract from face-to-face relationships, "Enhancing Reality" seeks to redefine the role of digital platforms in our lives as supportive rather than central.

The Role of Virtual Connections: Valuing online relationships while prioritizing physical-world interactions.

Here, the discussion pivots to understanding the unique benefits and limitations of virtual connections. We acknowledge the value of the global village created by the internet, allowing for diverse interactions and the maintenance of long-distance relationships. However, this section also emphasizes the irreplaceable nature of in-person connections and the depth and richness they bring to our lives. Practical advice is given on how to balance and integrate online relationships with those in the physical world, ensuring that the latter are given priority and space to flourish. It's a call to view digital connections as bridges to human interaction rather than destinations in themselves, with personal anecdotes and research supporting the benefits of this approach.

iv. Establishing Digital Boundaries

Time Management in the Digital Age: Setting limits on technology use to free up time for analog pursuits.

This part of the chapter addresses the crucial role of time management in establishing a healthy relationship with technology. It presents strategies for setting clear boundaries around technology use, allowing for more time to be invested in offline activities that contribute to personal growth and happiness. The section offers guidance on creating and maintaining a schedule that dedicates specific times for digital engagement, ensuring that it does not encroach upon time reserved for hobbies, relaxation, and face-to-face interactions. Tools like app blockers, scheduled internet downtimes, and tech-free zones within the home are discussed, with examples of how they can be effectively implemented.

Privacy and Presence: Balancing connectivity with the need for privacy and uninterrupted personal time.

Focusing on the intersection of privacy and presence, this subsection delves into the importance of protecting personal space and time in an era of hyper-connectivity. It explores how being constantly connected can infringe on our privacy and interrupt the flow of daily life, detracting from the quality of our presence in any given moment. Readers will learn about the benefits of disconnecting and how to establish privacy settings that safeguard their time and attention. By creating a personal protocol for digital engagement that respects one's privacy, individuals can cultivate a sense of presence that allows for more meaningful and focused engagement with the world around them. Techniques for negotiating digital boundaries with friends, family, and colleagues are also shared, ensuring that these boundaries are respected and maintained.

v. Technology in Service of Productivity

Tools That Empower: Leveraging apps and platforms that genuinely increase efficiency and productivity.

This section acknowledges that while technology can be a distraction, it also offers tools that can significantly boost productivity when used judiciously. It guides readers through a selection process to identify apps and platforms that streamline workflows, facilitate project management, and enhance communication, discarding those that do not serve a purpose. By focusing on tools that align with one's specific productivity goals, individuals can transform their digital devices into powerful allies in the pursuit of efficiency. Case studies and testimonials illustrate how certain digital tools have revolutionized time management, task delegation, and information organization for individuals and teams.

Automation for Liberation: Automating menial tasks to focus on high-value, deeply engaging activities.

Automation has the potential to free up significant amounts of time by handling repetitive tasks that do not require human creativity or emotional intelligence. This subsection delves into the concept of using automation not just for the sake of technology, but as a means to liberate time for creative and meaningful work. It provides insights into the types of tasks that are ideal for automation and introduces readers to the software and methodologies that can help them automate effectively. Real-world examples showcase how automating mundane tasks has enabled professionals to dedicate more energy to strategic thinking, innovation, and impactful work, ultimately leading to increased job satisfaction and personal fulfillment.

vi. Education and Technology

Digital Learning with Limits: Embracing the benefits of e-learning while maintaining engagement with the physical world.

In this part of the chapter, the discussion pivots to the realm of education, highlighting the advantages and pitfalls of digital learning. While acknowledging the accessibility, personalization, and vast resources e-learning provides, it also emphasizes the necessity for setting boundaries. The text encourages incorporating digital learning as a complement to traditional methods rather than a wholesale replacement. It suggests strategies for balancing screen time with physical materials and in-person interactions, ensuring that students develop a well-rounded educational experience. The content also explores case studies where hybrid learning models have successfully combined digital convenience with the irreplaceable value of hands-on experiences.

Tech as an Educational Tool: Integrating technology in learning environments without it becoming the focal point.

Moving beyond the binary choice of digital versus traditional education, this section explores how technology can be harnessed as a tool to enhance learning without dominating it. It recommends ways to integrate tech to facilitate exploration, collaboration, and creativity in learning, providing examples from cutting-edge educational institutions that have found an equilibrium. By integrating technology in a supportive role, educators can foster a learning environment that leverages digital tools for research, experimentation, and connectivity while ensuring that these tools do not overshadow the essential human elements of teaching and learning. Practical advice is offered for educators to critically assess educational tech, ensuring it serves pedagogical objectives and nurtures the development of critical thinking and problem-solving skills.

v. Health and Technology

Wearable Wellness: Utilizing health-tracking devices to promote well-being without becoming obsessed with data.

This subsection addresses the rise of wearable technology and its impact on our health routines. It emphasizes the benefits of devices that monitor physical activity, sleep patterns, and vital signs, offering insights into our health and encouraging more informed lifestyle choices. However, it also warns against the potential for data obsession, which can lead to anxiety and an unhealthy preoccupation with metrics. The narrative suggests ways to use wearables as tools for awareness and motivation, while advising readers to maintain a balanced perspective where personal intuition and well-being take precedence over numbers and charts.

Mental Health in the Digital Domain: Recognizing the impact of screen time on mental health and taking proactive steps to mitigate it.

In exploring the complex relationship between digital media consumption and mental health, this subsection delves into how prolonged screen time can affect mood, stress levels, and overall mental well-being. It discusses the subtle ways in which our digital habits can contribute to anxiety, depression, and feelings of inadequacy, especially through the lens of social media use. The text provides strategies for setting healthy digital boundaries, such as scheduling regular screen-free times, curating digital content to minimize exposure to negative stimuli, and using apps that monitor and restrict usage. It also touches on the importance of offline activities and real-world connections in maintaining mental balance, offering guidance for seeking a healthier digital life that supports rather than undermines mental health.

vi. Social Media with a Purpose

Constructive Sharing: Engaging in social media practices that foster positive connections and self-expression.

This subsection outlines a framework for utilizing social media in a way that contributes constructively to our lives and the lives of others. It promotes the idea of sharing content that is uplifting, informative, or expressive of one's genuine interests and passions, thereby creating a more positive digital environment. The approach advocates for mindfulness in the act of posting, encouraging users to consider the intent and potential impact of their shared content. The discussion extends to recognizing the power of social media as a tool for social change, community building, and personal growth when used with clear, positive intentions.

Filtering the Feed: Curating social media feeds to minimize negative content and maximize beneficial interactions.

This subsection deals with the practical steps users can take to actively shape their social media experience into one that enriches their life. It emphasizes the importance of being selective about who and what to follow, suggesting strategies for filtering out content that does not serve the user's well-being or align with their values. It talks about using features like muting, unfollowing, or blocking to remove toxic elements from the feed and employing algorithms to one's advantage by consciously engaging with content that is inspiring, educational, or conducive to well-being. The aim is to transform the social media feed into a source of inspiration, support, and positive reinforcement, rather than a trigger for stress or comparison.

vii. Ethical Technology Use

Sustainable Tech Practices: Making choices that support sustainability in technology use and disposal.

This segment addresses the environmental impact of our digital habits and the life cycle of the devices we use. It encourages readers to consider the carbon footprint of their online activities, the energy consumption of their devices, and the e-waste generated by discarded electronics. It offers guidance on reducing energy use, extending the lifespan of devices through maintenance and repair, and recycling old technology responsibly. This chapter aims to raise awareness of the ecological cost of our digital lives and provide practical steps for more sustainable technology use.

Digital Citizenship: Being responsible members of the online community and advocating for a kinder digital world.

Digital citizenship goes beyond just being savvy with technology; it's about understanding the social implications of our online actions. This section discusses the principles of ethical behavior in the virtual space, including respect for privacy, intellectual property rights, and the spread of misinformation. It underscores the importance of empathy in online interactions and the role each person plays in shaping the digital culture. This chapter also provides strategies for navigating online spaces with integrity, encouraging readers to foster communities that are inclusive, informed, and respectful.

viii. Embracing Technology as an Ally

As the chapter comes to a close, it calls for a redefined relationship with technology—one where gadgets and apps are not seen as masters of our attention, but as tools that serve our broader life goals. This concluding part reiterates that technology itself is neutral; it is the way we incorporate it into our lives that decides its impact. The text urges readers to exercise conscious choice in how they interact with digital devices and online spaces, ensuring these interactions enhance rather than detract from the quality of life.

The chapter challenges the reader to think of technology not as an overwhelming force but as a flexible instrument that can be molded to fit the contours of our human needs. It highlights the importance of using technology to amplify our capabilities, expand our horizons, and connect more deeply with the world around us. It encourages the adoption of a mindset that places technology in the role of a supportive partner in our quest for a meaningful and centered existence.

In conclusion, the chapter asserts that by setting boundaries, adopting ethical practices, and maintaining an awareness of our digital consumption, we can harness technology to enrich our lives without letting it dominate them. It calls for an ongoing dialogue about the role of technology in society, advocating for a future where digital advancement progresses hand-in-hand with human values. It is a future where technology, wielded with intention and care, becomes an ally in our endeavor to live fully, mindfully, and joyfully.

8

Community and Analog Anchoring

In an era of unprecedented digital connectivity, Chapter 8, "Community and Analog Anchoring," harkens back to the fundamental human need for physical community and shared experience. This chapter explores how, despite the convenience of digital interaction, there is an irreplaceable depth found in real-world connections. It outlines the ways in which communities built on analog interactions form the bedrock of our social fabric, providing a sense of belonging, understanding, and mutual support that virtual spaces can complement but not fully replace.

Here, we delve into the concept of 'Analog Anchoring', the practice of grounding community interactions in the physical world to strengthen bonds and build lasting relationships. The introduction sets the stage for a journey through various facets of community life that can benefit from a more tangible, less tech-driven approach. From community gardens to local book clubs, the chapter illustrates how analog activities foster a sense of place and presence, enabling people to connect on a level that transcends the superficial ties often formed online.

i. Building Robust Analog Communities Amidst Digital Ubiquity

Revitalizing the Modern Agora: Reimagining Public Spaces as Community Focal Points

This section delves into the transformative potential of public spaces when repurposed as dynamic community hubs in the fabric of our contemporary society. By drawing parallels with the ancient concept of the town square, it examines how these spaces can evolve beyond their traditional roles to become epicenters of community interaction, cultural exchange, and civic engagement in our digital age. The narrative unfolds through a detailed exploration of successful initiatives and design strategies that breathe new life into public venues—turning them into inclusive and vibrant locales that invite social interaction, collective celebration, and shared ownership among community members.

Catalyzing Connection Through Grassroots Initiatives and Local Meetups

Here, we cast a spotlight on the grassroots efforts that act as the lifeblood of community cohesion, illustrating how face-to-face meetups serve as powerful catalysts for forging deep social ties and igniting societal transformation. We provide a rich tapestry of stories and case studies that reveal the impact of organized local action and spontaneous group encounters in creating a sense of belonging and purpose. Through an in-depth look at diverse movements ranging from neighborhood gardening clubs to city-wide art projects, this section highlights the multifaceted ways in which these analog connections can nurture supportive networks, spur collaborative innovation, and promote a sense of agency and change that is often diluted in the virtual sphere.

ii. Shared Experiences: The Cornerstone of Human Connection

United in Elation and Adversity: The Indelible Bond of Collective Experiences

In this segment, we explore the profound psychological and sociological effects of communal experiences that take place in physical settings. The text delves into the rich tapestry of human emotions that collective activities evoke, from the heights of collective joy in festivals and celebrations to the solidarity found in communal challenges and protests. By contrasting these with the often-isolated nature of digital interaction, the narrative uncovers the unique ways in which shared physical spaces and events can forge strong bonds and a sense of unity among individuals. Stories and research illustrate how these lived experiences become part of our collective memory, shaping community identity and fostering resilience in the face of adversity.

Rituals and Traditions: Weaving the Social Fabric Through Time-Honored Practices

This section highlights the pivotal role that cultural and communal rituals play in sustaining and nurturing the social bonds within communities. It provides a contemplative analysis of how these time-honored practices serve as anchors for collective identity, transmitting values, and fostering a sense of continuity and belonging across generations. The discussion delves into a variety of cultural phenomena—from local festivities to national holidays—and examines how these rituals contribute to a shared understanding and communal narrative that digital interactions struggle to replicate. Through engaging storytelling and insightful commentary, the text invites readers to appreciate the enduring power of tradition and its irreplaceable role in maintaining the social fabric of communities in an increasingly digital world.

iii. Reclaiming Conversation in Public Spaces

Rediscovering the Human Dialogue: The Invaluable Art of Face-to-Face Conversation

Within this discourse, we turn our focus to the revitalization of face-to-face conversation as a foundational element of human connection. We dissect the subtle nuances and profound impacts of in-person dialogue, from the empathetic exchange of gazes to the unspoken language of body gestures, which enrich our understanding and foster deep connections. This section also addresses the challenges and opportunities presented by our current societal reliance on digital communication, positing the irreplaceable value of direct, physical conversation in building relationships, facilitating empathy, and nurturing our communal bonds.

Crafting Spaces for Serendipitous Encounters: The Role of Urban Design in Community Engagement

Expanding upon the concept of conversation, we examine how the built environment shapes our interactions and, by extension, our communities. Through case studies and expert insights, we delve into the principles of urban planning and public space design that are consciously crafted to encourage spontaneous social interactions among citizens. This part articulates the vision of cities and public venues as catalysts for community engagement, underlining the importance of creating spaces that invite gathering, dialogue, and the chance encounters that lead to lasting bonds and vibrant communities. It is an exploration of how thoughtful design can act as a silent conductor orchestrating the symphony of community life in the analog world.

iv. Civic Engagement: Participating Beyond the Screen

Grassroots Influence: The Vitality of Local Politics and Volunteering

In this in-depth exploration, we delve into the empowering realm of local politics and community volunteering. We dissect how personal involvement in these areas can lead to significant societal change and an enhanced sense of personal efficacy. This section presents a compelling narrative on the transformative power of grassroots initiatives and the intrinsic rewards of volunteer work. Readers will be guided through the process of becoming active participants in the governance of their communities and discover the profound impact that their collective actions can have on shaping the future of their local environments.

The Hub of Community Intelligence: Educational Workshops and Lifelong Learning

This segment celebrates the importance of lifelong learning and its embodiment in local workshops, seminars, and classes. It illustrates how community-based education acts not just as a repository of knowledge, but as a crucible for social cohesion and personal development. We emphasize the dual benefits of these analog educational forums: the acquisition of knowledge and the simultaneous forging of community ties. Detailed examples and success stories will showcase how educational initiatives serve as a linchpin for community engagement, offering avenues for individuals of all ages to continue growing intellectually while strengthening their connections within the community.

v. Community Supported Agriculture and Local Food Movements

From Farm to Table: The Community Connection

This section delves into the local food movement's ability to weave together a tapestry of community connections while bolstering the local economy. It reveals how the journey of food from farm to table embodies a narrative of care, dedication, and community spirit. Readers will gain insights into how participating in community-supported agriculture (CSA) programs not only provides them with fresh, seasonal produce but also embeds them within a cycle of mutual aid and economic support that benefits local farmers and consumers alike. The narrative explores the transformative effects these connections have on individuals' understanding of food, community responsibility, and ecological stewardship.

Food Cooperatives and Farmers' Markets: Pillars of a Healthy Community

This part celebrates the vital role of food cooperatives and farmers' markets as the bedrock of a health-conscious, sustainability-oriented community. It paints a vivid picture of these marketplaces as vibrant hubs where individuals converge not just to buy and sell but to exchange ideas, cultivate relationships, and reinforce communal bonds. The discussion extends to how these institutions act as accessible platforms for education on nutritional health and sustainable living, fostering a culture of shared learning and mutual support. By spotlighting various successful cooperatives and markets, the narrative underscores the profound impact these entities have in nurturing a sense of belonging and active participation in the community's well-being.

vi. The Role of Libraries and Community Centers

Libraries as Community Hubs: Beacons of Knowledge and Togetherness

This segment explores the transformation of libraries into dynamic community hubs that offer much more than books. It highlights how modern libraries have become inclusive sanctuaries for learning, creativity, and communal interaction, evolving to meet the diverse needs of their communities. From free educational programs to tech workshops, from art exhibitions to storytelling sessions for children, the library is presented as a microcosm of community life. The narrative illuminates the ways in which libraries facilitate knowledge sharing and access to information, fostering a culture of continuous learning and collective growth.

Revitalizing Community Centers: The Revival of the Commons

In this part, the focus shifts to the pivotal role that community centers play in revitalizing the concept of the commons in the 21st century. These centers are depicted as versatile, pulsating spaces that cater to a multitude of activities, groups, and interests. The discussion showcases the potential of community centers to act as engines for local development, offering resources ranging from sports facilities to arts and craft rooms, from event halls to maker spaces. It lays out a vision of these centers as platforms that encourage innovation, cultural expression, and social entrepreneurship, thereby cementing their status as cornerstones of a vibrant, connected, and resilient community.

vii. Analog Entertainment and Group Activities

Sports Leagues and Recreation Groups: Fostering Camaraderie through Physical Endeavor

This section delves into the community-building power of sports leagues and recreation groups. It celebrates the camaraderie and collective identity that emerge from team sports and group fitness activities. Illustrating both the health benefits and the social cohesion that such groups foster, the narrative highlights stories of individuals coming together to achieve common goals, support one another, and build friendships that extend beyond the playing field. The discourse champions the idea that through shared physical exertion and sportsmanship, diverse groups can find common ground and contribute to a more connected community.

Cultural Festivals and Live Performances: Celebrating Unity through the Arts

The transformative power of shared cultural experiences is the focal point of this segment. It paints a vibrant picture of how festivals and live performances become conduits for community engagement and joy. By gathering to appreciate the arts, communities strengthen their bonds and create shared memories that become part of their collective identity. The text takes the reader through various scenarios, from the electrifying atmosphere of music festivals to the intimate gatherings at local theater productions, emphasizing the way these events enrich community life, foster a sense of belonging, and celebrate human expression in its most palpable forms.

viii. Mindful Technology Use within Communities

Balancing Online and Offline Interactions: Harmonizing Digital and Analog Connections

In this discussion, we delve into how communities can skillfully balance the digital with the physical. This balance is crucial in maintaining the essence of human connection while still reaping the benefits of technological advancements. It outlines strategies for integrating digital tools in a way that complements rather than overpowers face-to-face interactions. By drawing on insights from sociologists, technologists, and community leaders, this section provides actionable advice on how to use technology to facilitate, rather than replace, real-world connections, ensuring that the heart of community remains rooted in the personal and tangible.

Tech-Free Zones and Times: Cultivating Presence and Participation

Exploring the concept of digital detox within the community fabric, this part of the chapter makes a case for intentional tech-free spaces and times. It argues for the health and social benefits of creating environments where individuals are encouraged to disconnect from their devices to foster mindfulness and present-moment awareness. Through interviews and case studies, it demonstrates how designated tech-free zones and periods not only enhance interpersonal connections but also boost mental well-being, creativity, and collective mindfulness. Practical guidelines for implementing these concepts in various community settings, such as schools, workplaces, and public spaces, are provided, illustrating a road map for communities to follow in their journey towards a more engaged and mindful way of living.

ix. Fostering Community Cohesion in the Digital Era

As this Chapter draws to a close, it encapsulates the essence of community as an interwoven tapestry of shared experiences, enriched by the palpable human connections that form within analog environments. This summation is a powerful call to action, urging communities to reclaim and reimagine their collective narratives in ways that honor and preserve the profundity of direct, physical interactions. It posits that while our digital advancements continue to evolve, they should serve as vessels that support—not supplant—the rich, sensorial experiences of the analog world.

The conclusion advocates for a conscious effort to maintain the equilibrium between digital convenience and analog depth. It emphasizes the irreplaceable nature of communal bonds forged through face-to-face encounters, hands-on activities, and shared physical spaces. The final words serve as a poignant reminder that in an increasingly virtual world, our commitment to the tangible aspects of life is what will sustain the core of community resilience and unity.

Readers are left with a reflective yet forward-looking message: As we navigate the complexities of modern life, let us leverage technology as a tool for enhancement rather than a replacement for the real-world fabric that connects us all. By doing so, we anchor our communities in the timeless and unyielding power of human presence, ensuring that, regardless of the digital tides, the essence of our collective spirit remains strong and vibrant.

9

The Future of Anchoring

As we sail through the tumultuous seas of the digital age, a horizon emerges where the cacophony of pings, notifications, and digital demands gives way to a post-digital burnout era—an era where the allure of always-on connectivity loses its grip and the yearning for authentic, grounded experiences becomes paramount. In Chapter 9, titled "The Future of Anchoring," we embark on a visionary exploration of what lies ahead for individuals, companies, and communities as they seek to redefine balance in an increasingly digitized world.

This chapter navigates the shifting tides, offering predictions and strategies for embracing a future that honors our intrinsic need for tangible connections and experiences—the anchors that keep us steadfast in our human essence. We will delve into how the landscapes of work, society, and personal life are poised to transform, and how we can proactively cultivate environments that foster deep-rooted well-being.

Navigating the Post-Digital Landscape

In the chapter section, we delve into the transformative shift that is occurring as society grapples with the repercussions of digital saturation. This era, marked by an overwhelming presence of technology in our daily lives, has begun to spur a counter-movement—a yearning for a return to simplicity and the authenticity of analog experiences.

The Awakening to Digital Oversaturation

The relentless flood of information in our digital era and the ever-present pressure to remain connected have culminated in a widespread state of collective fatigue. This phenomenon, increasingly recognized and discussed, is marked by a growing consciousness of the extensive toll that uninterrupted digital engagement exacts on various facets of human life.

i. Impact on Mental Health:

- *Cognitive Overload:* The human brain, faced with the ceaseless barrage of digital information, struggles to process and prioritize this influx, leading to cognitive overload. This can manifest as difficulty in concentration, decision-making fatigue, and increased susceptibility to stress and anxiety.
- *Diminished Attention Span:* Constant digital interruptions fragment our attention span, making it challenging to engage in deep, thoughtful work or maintain focus for extended periods.
- *Rise of Digital Anxiety:* The pressure to be perpetually available and responsive online has given rise to a phenomenon often termed 'digital anxiety', characterized by feelings of unease and restlessness associated with digital interactions or the fear of missing out (FOMO).

ii. Effects on Relationships:

- *Superficial Connections:* While digital platforms facilitate widespread connectivity, they often lead to more superficial interactions. The quality of relationships can suffer as the quantity of connections increases.

- *Erosion of Face-to-Face Communication Skills:* An overreliance on digital modes of communication is contributing to a decline in face-to-face communication skills, particularly among younger generations.
- *Neglect of Physical Presence:* The allure of the digital world can lead to the neglect of physically present relationships, impacting family dynamics and friendships.

iii. Overall Quality of Life:

- *Lifestyle Imbalance:* The encroachment of digital devices into all areas of life disrupts work-life balance, encroaches on leisure time, and can lead to unhealthy lifestyle habits.
- *Physical Health Impacts:* Extended screen time is linked to a range of physical health issues, including eye strain, poor posture, and disrupted sleep patterns.
- *Diminished Capacity for Solitude and Reflection:* The constant presence of digital devices can undermine our ability to enjoy solitude and engage in reflective thought, essential components for personal growth and mental well-being.

iv. Cultural and Societal Implications:

- *Normalization of Constant Connectivity:* Societal norms increasingly expect constant digital availability, reinforcing and perpetuating the cycle of digital fatigue.
- *Shifting Value Systems:* There is a shift in value systems, where digital prowess and presence are often prized over offline skills and achievements.

As awareness of these issues grows, there is a corresponding rise in movements advocating for a more balanced digital life. This includes digital detox initiatives, mindfulness practices focused on digital habits, and a broader societal conversation about recalibrating our relationship with technology. Recognizing the symptoms and consequences of this collective fatigue is the first step toward addressing its root causes and moving towards a healthier, more sustainable interaction with the digital world.

Rediscovery of the Analog as an Oasis

The recent resurgence in analog activities, characterized by their sensory richness and demand for focused presence, speaks to a deep-rooted human response to the saturation of digital technology in our lives. This trend, a counter-movement to our digital exhaustion, highlights a collective yearning for experiences that connect us more authentically with the physical world and our own senses.

i. Rediscovery of Vinyl Records:

- *Nostalgic Appeal:* The renewed interest in vinyl records is not just about nostalgia; it's about the tactile experience of handling the records, the ritual of playing them, and the rich, unfiltered sound they produce. This analog music experience offers a deeper engagement with art, contrasting with the often passive and distracted way digital music is consumed.

ii. Revival of Film Photography:

- *Intentionality in Art:* Film photography has witnessed a revival, especially among younger generations. This resurgence is driven by the desire for a more intentional and deliberate process of image creation, where each shot requires careful consideration, unlike the rapid, often thoughtless snapping enabled by digital cameras.

iii. Growth of Digital Detox Retreats:

- *Seeking Solitude and Focus:* The proliferation of digital detox retreats is a direct response to the constant connectivity of modern life. These retreats offer a haven where individuals can unplug from digital devices, re-engage with the natural world, and experience the benefits of undivided attention and quietude.

iv. Return to Physical Books:

- *The Joy of Reading:* Despite the convenience of e-books, many people are returning to physical books. The tactile sensation of turning pages, the smell of the paper, and the lack of digital distractions provide a more immersive reading experience.

v. Craftsmanship and DIY Culture:

- *Hands-On Creation:* The DIY movement and a renewed interest in craftsmanship reflect a desire to engage in creative, hands-on activities. From woodworking to knitting, these activities offer a sense of accomplishment and a physical connection to the creative process, which digital activities often lack.

vi. Board Games and Physical Play:

- *Social Interaction:* The resurgence of board games and other forms of physical play underscore the value of in-person social interaction. These activities encourage people to gather in a shared space, fostering a sense of community and connection.

vii. Mindful Practices:

- *Meditation and Yoga:* Mindful practices like meditation and yoga are gaining popularity as antidotes to the frenetic pace of digital life. They offer spaces of tranquility and introspection, allowing individuals to reconnect with themselves in a non-digital setting.

viii. The Pattern of Reaching for Simplicity:

- *This trend towards analog activities suggests a broader pattern:* in the face of overwhelming digitalization, there is an instinctual push towards simplicity and tangibility. As digital technology continues to permeate our lives, the appeal of analog experiences is likely to grow, serving as a grounding force and a reminder of the joys of the physical world.

In essence, the resurgence of these analog activities reflects a collective need to balance our digital consumption with experiences that ground us in the physical world. It's a reminder of the enduring value of sensory engagement and focused presence in an increasingly distracted digital landscape.

The Emergence of Slow Tech

The concept of "Slow Tech" emerges as a compelling response to the high-paced, often intrusive nature of modern digital technology. It represents a philosophy that seeks to realign technology's role in our lives, advocating for a design and usage approach that respects and enhances human rhythms, rather than disrupting them. Slow Tech is about fostering a harmonious relationship with our devices, where technology acts as a facilitator of well-being, rather than a constant source of interruption and distraction.

Core Principles of Slow Tech:

- *Intentionality and Mindfulness:* Slow Tech encourages users to engage with technology mindfully and intentionally. It promotes conscious decisions about when and how to use digital devices, favoring purposeful interaction over habitual use.
- *Design for Well-being:* This approach calls for technology to be designed with human well-being as a primary consideration. This includes user interfaces that reduce cognitive overload, features that encourage breaks, and functionality that aligns with natural human cycles, such as sleep patterns.
- *Sustainability:* Slow Tech aligns with sustainable practices, both in terms of environmental impact and long-term usability. It favors durable, quality devices that can be repaired and upgraded, reducing electronic waste and the constant churn of consumer electronics.
- *Encouraging Real-World Interaction:* Instead of technology that monopolizes attention, Slow Tech aims to complement and enhance real-world experiences. This includes technologies that encourage outdoor activities, face-to-face interactions, and engagement with the physical environment.

Examples of Slow Tech:

- *E-ink Devices:* Devices like e-readers use e-ink technology to mimic the experience of reading on paper, reducing eye strain and limiting distracting functionalities.
- *Digital Well-being Tools:* Features such as screen time trackers, notification silencers, and digital wellness apps that help users monitor and manage their digital consumption.

- *Mindfulness and Meditation Apps:* Applications designed to facilitate meditation, deep breathing, and mindfulness exercises, promoting mental relaxation and focus.
- *Smart Home Devices for Wellness:* Home technologies that adjust environmental factors like lighting and temperature in sync with natural circadian rhythms, supporting better sleep and relaxation.

Challenges and Considerations:

- While Slow Tech offers a promising direction, it faces challenges in widespread adoption, particularly in a market driven by rapid innovation and obsolescence. There's a need for consumer awareness and demand to shape industry practices.
- Accessibility and affordability are also crucial considerations. Slow Tech should be inclusive, offering solutions that cater to diverse economic and social groups.

In conclusion, Slow Tech is not a step backward from our digital advancements but a thoughtful recalibration of our relationship with technology. It's an invitation to harmonize our digital and analog lives, ensuring that our interactions with technology support our human needs for peace, presence, and uninterrupted time. As we continue to navigate the digital landscape, Slow Tech provides a guiding philosophy to ensure technology serves us, and not the other way around.

Cultural Shifts and Societal Adaptation

As societies grapple with the pervasive influence of digital technology, there's a growing movement towards cultural and societal adaptations that prioritize personal boundaries and genuine connections. These shifts reflect a broader reevaluation of how we integrate technology into our lives and communities, ensuring it serves to enhance, rather than diminish, our human experience. Here are various manifestations of these adaptations:

- *Urban Design for Interaction and Connection:*
  - Cities and towns are increasingly being designed or retrofitted to encourage more human interaction and less dependency on digital devices. This includes creating pedestrian-friendly spaces, community gardens, and public areas designed for people to meet and socialize, promoting a sense of community and belonging.
  - Architecture is incorporating more natural elements and communal spaces that encourage face-to-face interaction and activities away from screens.
- *Policies for Digital Well-being:*
  - Governments worldwide are implementing policies aimed at protecting digital privacy and regulating the amount of time spent on digital devices. For instance, laws around screen time in schools or the right to disconnect after work hours are becoming more common.
  - Regulatory bodies are also holding tech companies accountable for the societal impact of their products, encouraging them to design with ethics and well-being in mind.
- *Corporate Responsibility and Ethical Technology:*
  - There's a rising expectation for corporations to act responsibly in their deployment of technology. This includes ethical considerations in AI, transparency in data usage, and designing products that encourage healthy usage patterns.
  - Companies are increasingly adopting Corporate Social Responsibility (CSR) initiatives that address the digital well-being of both their employees and the wider community.
- *Educational Shifts towards Digital Literacy and Ethics:*

- Educational systems are adapting to not only teach digital skills but also foster digital literacy, which includes understanding the ethical implications of technology, the importance of digital privacy, and strategies for managing digital consumption.
- Schools and universities are incorporating lessons on building healthy digital habits, ensuring that the next generation is better equipped to navigate the digital world consciously and responsibly.

- *Community-Driven Digital Initiatives:*
  - Communities are forming groups and initiatives aimed at creating a healthier digital environment. This includes tech-free zones, digital detox retreats, and community events that encourage unplugging and reconnecting with the physical world.
  - Local businesses and organizations are increasingly supporting these initiatives, recognizing the value of a well-balanced community.

- *Revival of Analog Activities:*
  - There's a noticeable trend in the revival of analog hobbies and activities. From vinyl record collecting to film photography, people are increasingly seeking out activities that provide a tactile, deeply engaging alternative to the digital routine.
  - Public and private spaces are offering more opportunities for these analog experiences, such as workshops, clubs, and festivals that celebrate traditional crafts, arts, and cultural practices.

- *Healthcare Emphasis on Digital Health:*
  - The healthcare industry is increasingly recognizing the impact of digital lifestyles on physical and mental health. There's a growing focus on treating conditions related to

digital overuse and providing services that help individuals manage their digital consumption.

- *Advocacy and Public Awareness Campaigns:*
  - ○ Advocacy groups and public campaigns are raising awareness about the importance of digital well-being. These campaigns provide resources and support for individuals looking to balance their digital and analog lives, promoting a cultural shift towards more mindful technology use.

These adaptations across various sectors of society signify a collective move towards environments that respect personal boundaries and foster genuine human connections. By reevaluating and reshaping our relationship with technology, we can create a future that embraces the benefits of digital innovation while maintaining our well-being and societal values.

Mindful Consumption of Technology:

There is a burgeoning trend towards more mindful consumption of technology, where individuals take control of their digital lives by setting boundaries and cultivating a more discerning approach to technology use. This includes curating digital content consumption, setting aside specific times for technology use, and being more conscious of the quality and intention behind each interaction.

In summary, "Navigating the Post-Digital Landscape" invites readers to consider a future where the digital world is not shunned but rather integrated into our lives in a way that preserves space for the non-digital. It's a call to action for a balanced life, where technology serves as a tool rather than a tyrant, and where the richness of analog experiences is woven into the fabric of our daily existence.

Reimagining Workspaces

"Reimagining Workspaces" delves into a forward-looking analysis of how the pervasive issue of digital burnout is influencing the reinvention of work environments and corporate cultures. As we venture deeper into the 21st century, businesses are increasingly aware of the toll that constant connectivity and digital overload can take on their employees. This section of the chapter projects how companies might respond to these challenges by reshaping their physical and cultural landscapes to promote a healthier, more balanced approach to work.

The Evolution of Office Design: Businesses are predicted to evolve beyond the open-plan spaces that dominated the early 2000s, moving towards environments that offer a mix of solitude and community. Workspaces may become more modular, allowing employees to customize their surroundings to fit the task at hand—be it collaborative, creative, or contemplative work.

Integrating Nature and Well-Being: Biophilic design principles, which incorporate natural elements into the workplace to reduce stress and improve cognitive function, are expected to gain prominence. Features such as indoor plants, natural lighting, and even outdoor work areas could become standard as businesses recognize the productivity and wellness benefits.

Prioritizing Focus and Deep Work: Companies might adopt policies and design workspaces that help employees engage in deep work, minimizing digital interruptions. Soundproof pods, designated "focus zones," and scheduled quiet times could be instituted to help workers concentrate without the constant ping of emails and messages.

Cultures of Connection and Accessibility: In the post-digital burnout era, there's likely to be a shift towards creating work cultures that emphasize human connection. This could manifest in the form of more communal spaces for social interaction, scheduled group activities, and opportunities for in-person mentoring and collaboration.

Flexible Work Arrangements: Flexible work arrangements, including remote work options and adjustable hours, may become more than a perk—they could be integral to company policy. This shift acknowledges the varied rhythms of productivity and the need for work-life balance, which are essential for preventing burnout.

Tech-Free Zones and Digital Mindfulness: Anticipating a surge in the importance of digital mindfulness, businesses might establish tech-free zones or times, encouraging employees to disconnect and recharge. Companies may provide training on how to use technology mindfully to enhance productivity while avoiding digital fatigue.

Rethinking Performance Metrics: The way businesses measure success and productivity might change, with a move away from metrics that value always-on availability and toward those that recognize the quality of work and innovation. This reevaluation could lead to a healthier, more sustainable pace of work.

Investment in Employee Growth: Finally, companies may invest more in the continuous growth of their employees, providing resources for both professional and personal development. This could include workshops on analog skills, creativity retreats, and opportunities for sabbaticals to pursue personal projects.

"Reimagining Workspaces" anticipates a transformative shift in how businesses operate, with a newfound emphasis on creating work environments that nurture focus, creativity, and human connection. These changes represent a collective response to digital burnout and a commitment to fostering a workforce that is both productive and well.

Rethinking Community Infrastructure

"Rethinking Community Infrastructure" delves into a thoughtful exploration of the future transformation of public spaces and community infrastructures. It forecasts how urban planning, architectural design, and community initiatives will evolve to meet the human need for connection, collaboration, and shared real-world experiences. This part of the chapter suggests a future where our communal environments are intentionally crafted to counterbalance the isolating effects of digital saturation and to rekindle the intrinsic human desire for physical presence and togetherness.

Human-Centric Urban Design: The section predicts a shift towards urban design principles that prioritize human interaction and accessibility. It envisions cities and towns with more pedestrian zones, community gardens, and public squares that invite spontaneous gatherings and a sense of belonging. Planners and architects are expected to create spaces that are not just functional but also conducive to community life and well-being.

Multifunctional Public Spaces: The future could see the rise of versatile public spaces that can be adapted for various community needs—be they markets, performances, workshops, or social gatherings. Libraries might host maker spaces and local art exhibits, while parks could be designed to accommodate fitness classes, open-air theaters, and cultural festivals.

Reviving Local Economies: Community infrastructure planning is anticipated to focus on reviving local economies. This might involve supporting small businesses and startups through the establishment of incubators and shared workspaces that encourage local entrepreneurship and foster a sense of communal achievement.

Integration of Nature and Sustainability: There will be a concerted effort to integrate nature into community spaces, not just for aesthetic purposes but to promote sustainability and environmental stewardship. The chapter foresees green rooftops, urban forests, and eco-friendly buildings becoming commonplace, serving as daily reminders of the role communities play in the larger ecosystem.

Community-Driven Development: Community infrastructure is likely to be shaped increasingly by the voices of the residents themselves, with a greater emphasis on participatory design processes. This means more town hall meetings, community surveys, and platforms for residents to contribute ideas on how to make their living spaces more engaging and interconnected.

Spaces for Civic Engagement: Expectations are that public spaces will be explicitly designed to encourage civic engagement and social action. From public art that sparks conversation to arenas that host town meetings and educational seminars, the goal will be to create environments where democracy and community input are visibly valued and promoted.

Technological Integration with Mindfulness: While the emphasis is on analog interactions, technology will not be abandoned but integrated thoughtfully into public spaces. Wi-Fi in parks, interactive information kiosks, and smart lighting can enhance the usability and safety of community spaces without detracting from their role as places for human connection.

Transportation as a Community Experience: The section also anticipates changes in public transportation, envisioning it as a seamless, enjoyable, and community-oriented experience. This could include redesigns of transit hubs to serve as pleasant, multifunctional spaces where community members can shop, relax, and interact while on their daily commute.

In conclusion, "Rethinking Community Infrastructure" offers a vision of future spaces that are rooted in the physical and social fabric of community life. It reflects a conscious move towards designing and using our environments to foster the shared experiences that are essential for a thriving, connected society.

Education for the Future: A Holistic Approach in a Digital Era

The future of education demands a nuanced approach that interweaves digital fluency with critical thinking, hands-on learning, and emotional intelligence. Here's a detailed exploration of how educational systems can evolve to meet these needs:

- *Digital Fluency and Critical Thinking:*
  - Integrating Technology with Reasoning: Schools will not only teach students how to use technology but also how to critically assess and leverage it. This involves

understanding algorithms, data analysis, and the underlying mechanisms of technology.

- Encouraging Digital Literacy: Students will learn not just to consume digital content, but to create and critique it, understanding its impact on society and individual perceptions.

- *Hands-on Learning:*
  - Project-Based Learning (PBL): A shift towards PBL where students solve real-world problems through research, collaboration, and building actual solutions.
  - STEAM Approaches: Emphasis on Science, Technology, Engineering, Arts, and Mathematics (STEAM) to foster creativity and innovation.

- *Emotional Intelligence:*
  - Curriculum for Self-Awareness: Schools will incorporate emotional intelligence as a key component of the curriculum, helping students to understand and manage their own emotions and those of others.
  - Social-Emotional Learning (SEL): Programs aimed at developing empathy, resilience, and communication skills will be standard, preparing students for the emotional complexities of the modern world.

- *Balancing Screen Time:*
  - Awareness and Moderation: Educators will teach the importance of balancing screen time with physical activity and face-to-face interactions.
  - Tech-Free Zones: Implementing tech-free times or zones within schools to encourage students to engage with the physical world and each other.

- *Critical Media Literacy:*
  - Understanding Media Bias: Students will learn to identify biases and differentiate between misinformation, disinformation, and credible information.

- Navigating the Information Landscape: Skills to navigate the vast information landscape critically, discerning the quality and validity of information sources.
- *Global Citizenship:*
  - Cultural Competency: Education will emphasize global awareness and cultural competency, acknowledging the connected nature of our digital world.
  - Ethical Considerations: Discussions around the ethics of technology, privacy, digital footprints, and the global impact of individual and collective digital practices.
- *Adaptive Learning Technologies:*
  - Customized Learning Experiences: Use of AI and machine learning to tailor education to individual student needs, styles, and paces.
  - Data-Driven Insights: Leveraging data analytics to enhance learning outcomes and provide personalized feedback to students and educators.
- *Teacher Training and Support:*
  - Professional Development: Continuous professional development for educators in the latest educational technologies and methodologies.
  - Support Systems: Increased support for teachers, including access to digital resources and collaboration tools to share best practices.
- *Policy and Infrastructure:*
  - Investment in EdTech: Strategic investment in educational technology that supports these multifaceted learning objectives.
  - Equitable Access: Policies to ensure all students have equal access to the technology and resources they need to succeed.
- *Parent and Community Engagement:*

- ○ Community Involvement: Stronger partnerships between schools, parents, and communities to support learning objectives.
- ○ Lifelong Learning: Encouraging a culture of lifelong learning that extends beyond the classroom and traditional school years.

The future of education lies in its ability to adapt to the changing landscape, where technology is a tool for enhancing learning, not the end goal. By fostering an education system that values digital skills alongside critical thinking, practical skills, and emotional intelligence, we can prepare students not just for the job market, but for life in a complex, highly interconnected world.

The New Consumer Consciousness

"The New Consumer Consciousness" is an insightful examination of the evolving values of consumers in the age of information and environmental awareness. This section probes into the collective shift towards more sustainable, private, and authentic modes of consumption and how modern companies are recalibrating their strategies in response.

Emergence of Ethical Consumerism: The narrative explores how a growing number of consumers are making purchasing decisions based on ethical considerations. These consumers are looking beyond the product to the practices of the companies behind them—how they source materials, treat their workers, and contribute to the community. This shift is pressing companies to not only publicize their corporate social responsibility efforts but to embed these practices into their core business strategies.

Demand for Transparency and Authenticity: Consumers are increasingly skeptical of traditional advertising and are demanding greater transparency from brands. This section predicts a rise in the importance of authenticity and storytelling in marketing, where the focus is on building trust through honest communication and by demonstrating commitment to values that resonate with the customer base.

Privacy as a Priority: In the wake of numerous data breaches and privacy scandals, privacy has become a significant concern for consumers. The chapter discusses how companies are responding by making data protection a key feature of their products and services. This includes more transparent data usage policies and offering customers greater control over their personal information.

Sustainable Choices and Circular Economy: There is a growing consumer appetite for sustainable products and business models that support the circular economy. The chapter delves into how companies are innovating to meet this demand, whether through developing new materials that are more environmentally friendly, adopting zero-waste manufacturing processes, or creating platforms for product life extension, such as repair services and secondary markets.

Local and Community-Focused Commerce: The chapter envisions a resurgence of local and community-focused commerce as consumers seek to support their local economies and reduce the environmental impact of their purchases. It predicts an increase in the popularity of farmers' markets, local craft fairs, and other community-centric retail experiences that also serve as social gathering points.

Personalization and Co-Creation: With advancements in technology, personalized products and services are becoming the norm. Consumers are not just passive recipients; they are active participants in the creation process. The section foresees companies offering more opportunities for customization, allowing consumers to be part of the design process, thereby increasing engagement and loyalty.

Wellness and Well-being: Consumers are increasingly investing in their health and well-being, and companies are responding with products and services that promise to enhance quality of life. This extends beyond physical health products to include mental and emotional well-being offerings, such as mindfulness apps, wellness retreats, and even workplaces designed to reduce stress and promote health.

Technology with a Human Touch: Finally, as technology becomes ever more pervasive, there is a counter-movement of consumers seeking technology that feels more human and less intrusive. This trend is pushing companies to develop technology that is intuitive, unobtrusive, and which enhances rather than dominates everyday life.

In conclusion, "The New Consumer Consciousness" portrays a dynamic shift in consumer values that is driving businesses to adapt and innovate. It heralds a future where commerce is not only about the exchange of goods but about meaningful experiences, sustainable practices, and a deeper engagement with the ethical dimensions of production and consumption.

Mental Health and Digital Well-being

The section delves into the increasingly pivotal role of mental health awareness in shaping our interactions with technology. It brings to light the growing trend towards digital detoxes, the burgeoning market for mindfulness applications, and the development of wellness-focused technology aimed at fostering mental and emotional well-being.

Understanding the Impact of Digital Overload: Here, the text unpacks how constant connectivity and the influx of information can lead to digital fatigue, stress, and a decline in mental health. It provides insights into the science behind screen time and its effects on the brain, sleep patterns, and overall well-being, encouraging a nuanced understanding of digital consumption's implications.

The Emergence of Digital Detox Initiatives: This part of the chapter surveys the increasing popularity of digital detoxes, where individuals consciously refrain from using electronic devices for a certain period to reduce stress and improve quality of life. It looks at organized retreats, personal strategies, and community campaigns that promote regular intervals of disconnection to restore balance.

Mindfulness Goes Digital: Despite the irony, this section explores how technology itself is being leveraged to combat the very issues it sometimes creates. It highlights the proliferation of mindfulness and meditation apps that aim to make mental health care more accessible, offering guided practices, stress-reduction techniques, and habit-forming activities that encourage users to develop mindfulness as a daily routine.

Wellness-Focused Tech Innovations: The narrative turns to innovative technologies designed with mental health in mind. From wearables that track stress levels and suggest interventions, to AI-driven mental health platforms that offer cognitive behavioral therapy—this part demonstrates how technology is becoming an ally in the quest for better mental health.

The Role of Social Media Platforms: Acknowledging the mixed role of social media in mental well-being, this segment delves into the initiatives platforms are taking to reduce negative impacts on mental health, such as features that remind users to take breaks, tools for reporting and managing cyberbullying, and algorithms that aim to promote content that can have a positive psychological impact.

Corporate Responsibility and Employee Well-being: The chapter also casts a spotlight on how corporations are incorporating mental health into digital policies. It reviews corporate wellness programs that limit after-hours communication, encourage digital breaks, and provide digital well-being training to employees, showcasing a shift in how companies value mental health.

Educational Efforts for Responsible Tech Use: Finally, there is a discussion on educational initiatives aimed at equipping individuals, especially the younger generation, with the skills to navigate the digital world responsibly. This includes school curriculums on digital citizenship, programs on managing digital footprints, and fostering an understanding of how to maintain a healthy balance between online and offline worlds.

"Mental Health and Digital Well-being" reflects a growing consciousness about the importance of maintaining psychological health in the digital age. It emphasizes proactive measures and the adoption of technologies that support mental health, proposing a future where our digital lives are managed in harmony with our intrinsic need for mental well-being.

Policy and Advocacy for Balanced Tech Use

In the section, we delve into the proactive measures that can be taken to construct a sustainable and ethical technological environment that respects human well-being. The emphasis is on the need for comprehensive policies and vigorous advocacy to steer the role of technology in society towards a more balanced and humane direction.

Crafting Guidelines for Ethical Design: The discussion begins with the imperative for industry-wide standards that mandate ethical design practices. It underscores the necessity for technology developers to incorporate features that mitigate the risk of addiction and prioritize user well-being. This could mean designing applications that encourage breaks, or systems that provide more transparent user information regarding time spent on devices.

Legislative Actions for Protecting Digital Consumers: Here, the narrative shifts to the legislative arena, advocating for laws that protect users from the potentially harmful effects of technology. The writer would call for regulations that ensure companies are transparent about data collection, consent, and the psychological strategies employed in user interface design that may lead to compulsive use.

Supporting Digital Literacy and Education: The text also highlights the role of education in equipping individuals with the skills to navigate the digital landscape responsibly. Policies that integrate digital literacy into school curriculums can empower younger generations to understand the nature of the digital world, discern the quality of information, and manage their digital footprints with care.

Advocacy Groups and Consumer Awareness: The writer emphasizes the role of advocacy groups in driving consumer awareness and influencing policy. By mobilizing public opinion and pressuring corporations and governments, these groups can be instrumental in catalyzing change. They can also play a crucial role in spreading awareness about the importance of balanced tech use and supporting initiatives that aim to reduce the negative impacts of technology on society.

Public Health Campaigns: Exploring the public health perspective, the section suggests campaigns similar to those used in anti-smoking efforts to raise awareness about the health impacts of excessive tech use. It suggests that informing the public about the potential risks and providing guidelines for healthier technology consumption can lead to more mindful use patterns.

Incentivizing Responsible Tech Development: The conversation turns towards the potential for incentivizing companies to develop more responsible technology. This could involve tax benefits, awards, or public recognition for companies that implement and adhere to ethical design principles.

International Collaboration for Global Standards: Given the global reach of technology, the writer argues for international collaboration to set global standards for balanced tech use. This would involve cross-border efforts to tackle issues like digital addiction, misinformation, and online privacy.

In sum, the "Policy and Advocacy for Balanced Tech Use" section envisions a future where concerted efforts from governments, industry, advocacy groups, and consumers foster a tech ecosystem that prioritizes human welfare. As the writer, I advocate for a multifaceted approach that combines education, regulation, and incentivization to champion a balanced and conscious engagement with technology.

Innovating for Intentionality

The section casts a spotlight on the emerging paradigm where companies and technological innovators are recalibrating their focus to create products that enrich lives without leading to an overwhelming dependence on technology. It celebrates a new wave of innovation that's anchored in the principles of intentional use, purpose, and user empowerment.

Design Philosophy Shift: The narrative begins by detailing the fundamental shift in design philosophy that's taking root in some forward-thinking tech companies. It describes a movement away from persuasive design that hooks users to a more ethical approach focused on enhancing user autonomy and decision-making. This approach entails building products that users can engage with on their own terms, facilitating a healthier relationship with technology.

Tech That Encourages Digital Wellness: The writer examines the influx of apps and devices that actively promote digital wellness. These might include applications that monitor device usage and encourage breaks, or devices that are intentionally limited to discourage constant engagement. For instance, e-ink readers that prevent multimedia distractions, or smartphones with features that promote periods of disconnection, would be highlighted.

Mindful Metrics and Analytics: This part of the discussion introduces companies that are developing analytics tools designed to provide users with insights into their digital habits, rather than simply driving up engagement metrics. By offering a transparent overview of how individuals interact with technology, these tools can help users make informed decisions about their digital consumption.

Intentionality in User Experience (UX) Design: Here, the focus turns to UX design principles that prioritize user intentionality. It features UX strategies that prompt users to reflect on their technology use, such as reminder prompts that question if the user truly wants to spend more time on a task, or notification settings that users can customize to fit their personal goals and schedules.

Smart Environments that Adapt: The section delves into the concept of smart environments that adapt to support user intentionality. For example, smart homes that learn a user's routines and help foster productive habits, or office spaces that adjust lighting and temperature to optimize focus and reduce digital strain.

Tools for Focus and Productivity: Attention is given to productivity tools designed with intentionality at their core. These include apps that help users manage tasks with efficiency, filter out distractions, and enable deeper work sessions. Tools that utilize artificial intelligence to understand a user's workflow and suggest personalized strategies for more intentional work would also be discussed.

Hardware that Supports Purposeful Engagement: Finally, the writer highlights hardware innovations that support intentional engagement with technology, such as wearables that remind users to engage with the physical world, or modular devices that users can customize to align with their specific needs and avoid feature overload.

In conclusion, "Innovating for Intentionality" paints a hopeful picture of the future, where technology is a facilitator of human potential and well-being. The writer showcases how a cross-section of companies and technologies are leading the charge in ensuring that the tools we use are designed with the well-being of the user as the prime directive, ultimately allowing for a more intentional, purpose-driven life.

10

The Global Implications

Global Perspectives on Digital Saturation and the Quest for Balance

As digital technology permeates every corner of the globe, different cultures are grappling with its pervasive presence and seeking ways to maintain a harmonious digital-analog existence. This exploration reveals the myriad approaches societies are taking to cultivate equilibrium in an increasingly connected world.

- *The Nordic Embrace of 'Lagom':*
  - In countries like Sweden, the concept of 'Lagom' — meaning 'just the right amount' — is being applied to digital consumption. This cultural ethos advocates for a moderate approach, where technology is used purposefully and in balance with offline life.
- *Japan's 'Moratorium':*
  - Japanese culture, with its deep roots in mindfulness and tradition, fosters 'Moratorium' periods where digital devices are set aside to engage in reflective practices like tea ceremonies, which emphasize the here and now.
- *India's Digital Detox Retreats:*

- Leveraging its rich heritage of spirituality, India offers digital detox retreats that blend ancient practices like yoga and meditation with modern wellness trends, encouraging individuals to disconnect from technology and reconnect with their inner selves.

- *Germany's 'Feierabend':*
  - Many German companies promote 'Feierabend,' a tradition of respecting personal time after work where employees are encouraged to unplug from digital work communications, thereby fostering a clear distinction between work and leisure.

- *Bhutan's Gross National Happiness:*
  - In Bhutan, the measure of Gross National Happiness over GDP has influenced how technology is integrated into society. Policies and practices are crafted to ensure that technological progress supports societal well-being rather than detracting from it.

- *The South Korean Balance of Screen and Green:*
  - South Korea, despite being one of the most connected societies, is pioneering 'screen and green' initiatives, establishing parks and green spaces where screens are discouraged, thus promoting interactions with nature.

- *Brazil's Tech-Free Carnaval:*
  - During festivals like Carnaval, Brazilians are known to immerse themselves fully in the celebrations, setting aside digital devices to engage deeply with the music, dance, and communal revelry, celebrating the joy of collective experience.

- *Silicon Valley's Analog Counter-Culture:*
  - Interestingly, in the heart of the digital revolution, there is a growing counter-culture where tech leaders send their children to schools with low-tech education models, emphasizing hands-on learning and human interaction.

- *French 'Digital Dieting':*
  - France has introduced legal measures to curb digital encroachment into personal life, including the 'right to disconnect' laws, which empower employees to step away from work-related technology outside of business hours.
- *New Zealand's Digital Inclusivity:*
  - With a focus on inclusivity, New Zealand implements programs ensuring all segments of society have access to technology, but with a strong emphasis on community engagement and the preservation of Maori cultural values in the digital realm.
- *Canada's Indigenous Connectivity:*
  - Canada has initiatives that use technology to connect indigenous communities, not only bringing digital infrastructure to remote areas but also supporting the preservation of languages and traditions through digital means.

Each culture's unique strategies reflect a shared human desire for balance in the face of digital omnipresence. Whether through legislative action, societal norms, or individual lifestyle choices, these diverse practices offer valuable insights into the universal quest to navigate the complexities of the digital age while preserving the essence of our analog humanity. Through these lenses, we can glimpse a mosaic of potential paths toward a future where technology serves as a bridge to greater well-being rather than a barrier to authentic connection.

Cultural Responses to Digital Saturation: Navigating the Complexities of a Connected World

The phenomenon of digital saturation — the all-encompassing infusion of digital technology into everyday life — has become a defining feature of modern society. As communities around the globe confront the repercussions of this digital omnipresence, varied cultural responses have emerged, reflecting deep-seated values and the adaptive capacities of societies. This section provides an overview of how different cultures are addressing the challenges and opportunities presented by digital saturation.

- *The Search for Digital Equilibrium:*
  - Across cultures, there is a growing recognition of the need to find an equilibrium that allows for the benefits of digital advancements while mitigating their potential harms. This search for balance is leading to a reevaluation of how we interact with technology on a societal level.
- *Societal Reflections and Reactions:*
  - The impact of digital saturation has prompted introspection about what it means to live well in the digital age. This includes discussions around privacy, the nature of work, mental health, and the quality of interpersonal relationships.
- *Cultural Renaissance in Digital Adaptation:*
  - Some societies have turned to their cultural roots to find solutions, resulting in a kind of renaissance where traditional practices are reimagined in the context of the digital world. This fusion of the old and new is producing unique ways of incorporating technology into cultural practices.
- *Preservation of Analog Values:*
  - Amidst the digital wave, there is a concerted effort to preserve analog values such as face-to-face communication, communal gatherings, and unplugged leisure activities. This preservation is not just about nostalgia but about maintaining a sense of human connection and identity.
- *Innovative Policy Responses:*
  - Governments have begun crafting innovative policies to address digital saturation. This includes initiatives to

protect digital rights, manage screen time in schools, and promote digital literacy that empowers citizens to use technology wisely.

- *Community-Driven Tech Solutions:*
  - At a community level, there are movements towards developing technology solutions that are driven by community needs and values, rather than solely commercial interests. This includes community-owned networks, local content creation, and platforms that prioritize communal welfare.
- *Global Dialogues and Exchange:*
  - There is an increasing global dialogue about digital saturation, with international conferences, online forums, and cross-cultural exchanges helping to share insights and strategies. These global conversations facilitate the exchange of best practices and offer solidarity in the face of shared challenges.
- *Redefining Success in the Digital Age:*
  - Definitions of success and progress are being redefined, with metrics expanding beyond GDP and productivity to include well-being, sustainability, and the quality of social interactions.
- *The Role of Education and Mentorship:*
  - Educational institutions and mentorship programs are adapting curricula and guidance to prepare the next generation for a world where digital and analog coexist. This includes teaching critical thinking about technology use and fostering skills for digital resilience.
- *Artistic and Literary Reflection:*
  - Artists and writers are exploring the themes of digital saturation in their work, providing commentary and raising public awareness about its implications. These cultural artifacts are essential for understanding and processing the collective experience of a digitally saturated society.

As we delve into the specific cultural responses, we observe not just a reaction to digital saturation, but a proactive shaping of the digital landscape to align with diverse cultural values and aspirations. These responses offer a panoramic view of humanity's resilience and creativity in the face of a rapidly changing technological environment.

Technology and Cultural Values: Aligning Digital Practices with Inherent Philosophies

In a world where digital technologies are deeply embedded in the fabric of daily life, cultural values and philosophies significantly influence how different societies engage with and regulate these tools. From the Scandinavian ideal of 'lagom' to the Japanese principle of 'wabi-sabi', traditional concepts shape modern digital practices.

- *Scandinavia and 'Lagom': The Pursuit of Balance*
  - In Scandinavian cultures, 'lagom' — a term that connotes balance, moderation, and sufficiency — permeates lifestyle choices, including technology use. This cultural inclination towards equilibrium drives Scandinavians to adopt a more measured and intentional approach to digital tools, seeking to enhance life without allowing technology to dominate.
- *Japan and 'Wabi-Sabi': Embracing Imperfection*
  - The Japanese aesthetic of 'wabi-sabi', which finds beauty in imperfection and transience, informs the national dialogue on technology. It encourages a respectful and mindful engagement with digital tools, prioritizing harmony and the appreciation of technology as an impermanent, though valuable, aspect of life.
- *Bhutan and Gross National Happiness*
  - Bhutan's unique development philosophy, which measures progress through Gross National Happiness rather than

GDP, extends to its technological policies. The country advocates for a cautious and selective integration of technology that upholds social well-being and communal values.

- *Germany and 'Datenschutz': The Right to Privacy*
  - Germany's strong emphasis on 'Datenschutz' (data protection) reflects a cultural valuation of privacy and individual rights. This has led to stringent policies governing digital data and a public that is more conscious of privacy issues associated with technology use.
- *India's 'Jugaad' Innovation*
  - In India, 'jugaad' — a term used to describe a frugal and flexible approach to problem-solving — shapes its technological landscape. It is reflected in the way technology is adapted and repurposed to meet diverse needs across varied socioeconomic spectra, often leading to innovative and resourceful use of digital tools.
- *Brazil's 'Jeitinho' and Social Connectivity*
  - The Brazilian concept of 'jeitinho', which translates to finding a way to accomplish something despite obstacles, often applies to the use of social media and digital platforms to overcome socio-economic barriers, fostering strong networks of support and connection.
- *United States and the Silicon Valley Ethos*
  - In the United States, particularly in Silicon Valley, there is a cultural valorization of innovation and disruption, which often drives a rapid and enthusiastic adoption of new technologies. However, this is counterbalanced by emerging movements that advocate for a more reflective and sustainable approach to technology development and use.
- *South Korea's Digital Ubiquity*
  - South Korea, known for its widespread digital connectivity, balances technological advancement with cultural norms that stress social cohesion and collective progress.

This balance is evident in their policies and educational systems that emphasize both technological skills and social etiquette.

- *Nordic Focus on Digital Welfare*
  - The Nordic countries, with their welfare state model, extend their focus on societal welfare to the digital domain, investing in public digital infrastructures that are accessible and designed with the user's well-being in mind.
- *New Zealand's 'Manaakitanga' and Online Communities*
  - 'Manaakitanga', a Maori term for hospitality and kindness, influences New Zealand's approach to online communities, advocating for digital spaces that are inclusive, respectful, and community-oriented.

Each culture's intrinsic values act as a compass guiding their collective and individual digital journeys. While technology itself is often seen as a universal language, the subtleties of cultural philosophies and values infuse it with local significance and shape its role in society. These diverse cultural prisms through which technology is viewed and utilized offer rich insights into the global tapestry of human-technology interaction.

Global Digital Habits: A Comparative Cultural Tapestry

In an age where digital connectivity transcends geographical boundaries, a comparative analysis of global digital habits reveals a fascinating mosaic of practices that are shaped by local customs, economic conditions, regulatory frameworks, and cultural nuances. Here's an exploration of how different regions engage with technology, highlighting both stark differences and intriguing commonalities.

- *Connectivity and Internet Usage Patterns*

- In regions like North America and Northern Europe, high-speed internet access is ubiquitous, leading to habits centered around constant connectivity and streaming services. In contrast, in parts of Africa and South Asia, intermittent access and lower bandwidths have given rise to the popularity of offline viewing options and data-light applications.

- *Social Media Engagement*
  - The use of social media varies widely. In East Asia, platforms like WeChat and LINE offer multifunctional ecosystems where social engagement is integrated with commerce and services. Meanwhile, in the Middle East, there's a high engagement in visual and video content on platforms like Instagram and Snapchat, often used to express individuality within a collective society.

- *E-commerce Behaviors*
  - While the convenience of online shopping is globally recognized, in places like Southeast Asia, social commerce via platforms like Facebook and Instagram is prevalent, blending social media use with shopping. In contrast, Western consumers often utilize established e-commerce giants such as Amazon and eBay.

- *Mobile Versus Desktop*
  - There's a pronounced preference for mobile devices over desktops in regions such as Sub-Saharan Africa and Latin America due to mobile's accessibility and affordability. However, in many Western countries, while mobile use is significant, desktops remain essential for professional and complex tasks.

- *Digital Payments and Banking*
  - Scandinavian countries lead in cashless payments, often seen as pioneers in embracing digital transactions. Conversely, in parts of Central Asia and the Middle East, cash

remains king, though there's a growing trend towards mobile banking solutions.

- *Work-Related Tech Use*
  - In the Silicon Valley-dominated tech sphere, there's a trend towards using digital tools for enhancing productivity. On the other hand, in countries like Japan, traditional business practices still hold significant sway, though digital tools are being slowly integrated.
- *Digital Entertainment*
  - Streaming services like Netflix and Spotify have global reach, yet local platforms in countries like India (Hotstar) and China (iQIYI) show that regional content and local language options can dominate market preferences.
- *Privacy and Security Concerns*
  - Europe's GDPR has set a high standard for digital privacy, influencing user habits towards greater awareness of data rights. In other parts of the world, such as in many Asian countries, there's a varied landscape of privacy concerns and practices, with some regions showing less public concern over data privacy.
- *Educational Technology*
  - There's a significant embrace of educational technologies in North America and parts of Asia, where there's a focus on individual learning. In contrast, in parts of Africa and South America, communal learning is more common, though digital tools are being introduced to enhance this collective educational experience.
- *Gaming Cultures*
  - Gaming is a global phenomenon but takes on local flavors. South Korea's gaming culture is heavily community-oriented with a vibrant esports scene, while in Western countries, there's a trend towards immersive single-player experiences.

By examining these digital habits, it becomes evident that there are threads of commonality, such as the universal appeal of connectivity and the convenience of digital transactions. Yet, the fabric of each society, woven from its unique cultural, economic, and political yarns, colors the way technology is adopted and utilized. This comparative analysis not only highlights the diversity of global digital practices but also underscores the adaptability of technology to serve different human needs and cultural contexts.

Lessons from Tech-Light Communities: Embracing Intentionality and Simplicity

In examining communities where technology is less pervasive, we uncover a wealth of insights into the ways life can be structured to prioritize direct human experience, community interaction, and environmental harmony. These communities, whether shaped by economic necessity, cultural traditions, or conscious choice, offer valuable lessons in the art of living a tech-light life.

- *Community and Connectivity*
  - In many tech-light communities, there's a stronger emphasis on face-to-face interactions and the development of tight-knit relationships. Without the distractions of constant digital connectivity, members often form deeper communal ties, fostering a sense of belonging and mutual support.
- *Time and Pace*
  - The absence or minimal presence of technology often results in a different perception of time. Life tends to be less hurried, and the pace of day-to-day activities is more reflective and deliberate. This slower pace can contribute to reduced stress levels and a greater appreciation for the present moment.

- *Sustainability and Resourcefulness*
  - Tech-light communities frequently exhibit a high degree of sustainability and resourcefulness. The limited use of digital devices reduces energy consumption and electronic waste, and the necessity breeds innovation, with individuals finding creative solutions for challenges that might otherwise be solved with digital technology.
- *Education and Learning*
  - Educational models in these communities typically focus on hands-on skills and oral traditions. Learning is often intergenerational, with knowledge being passed down through practical involvement and storytelling, which can provide a rich, contextual understanding of local history and life skills.
- *Entertainment and Play*
  - With limited access to digital entertainment, there's a strong culture of live, participatory forms of amusement such as storytelling, music, dance, and games. These activities not only provide entertainment but also serve to reinforce cultural traditions and community bonds.
- *Economic Models*
  - Economic transactions in tech-light communities are often based on trade, barter systems, or local currencies, fostering a local economy that supports direct exchanges of goods and services. This can lead to a more equitable distribution of resources and strengthen the local community.
- *Problem-Solving and Creativity*
  - Without the convenience of digital tools, individuals and communities become adept problem-solvers with a strong creative streak. There's an inherent innovation in how everyday challenges are approached, often leading to unique and sustainable solutions.

- *Health and Well-being*
  - Many tech-light communities enjoy benefits to physical and mental health by being more active, spending more time outdoors, and having fewer distractions and interruptions. This can lead to a more holistic approach to health and well-being.
- *Spirituality and Reflection*
  - With more time for reflection and fewer external stimuli, individuals in tech-light communities may have a more contemplative lifestyle. This can foster a deep sense of spirituality or a profound connection with nature.
- *Resistance and Resilience*
  - Communities that have resisted the encroachment of pervasive digital technology often exhibit a strong sense of resilience. They have the ability to maintain their cultural values and lifestyles in the face of external pressures and are adept at navigating change on their own terms.

Incorporating these lessons from tech-light communities can inspire a more balanced approach to technology, reminding us that while digital tools can enhance our lives, they are not the sole pathway to fulfillment and community. The wisdom of these communities teaches us the value of intentionality, simplicity, and the irreplaceable quality of human and environmental connections.

National Policies on Digital Well-being: Global Initiatives to Counter Digital Overload

Around the world, governments are recognizing the need to address the impact of digital overload on the well-being of their citizens. Through innovative policies and initiatives, they aim to create healthier digital ecosystems and improve the quality of life. Here's a closer look at some of these strategies:

- *France's "Right to Disconnect"*
  - France has been a pioneer with its "right to disconnect" law, implemented in 2017. This legislation obliges companies with more than 50 employees to establish hours when staff should not send or answer emails. The move aims to combat the encroachment of work into personal time and reduce employee stress and burnout.
- *South Korea's Internet Dream Village Project*
  - To combat internet addiction among youths, South Korea launched the Internet Dream Village Project. This initiative offers children and teenagers a break from digital life by engaging them in outdoor activities and teaching them about life away from screens.
- *Canada's Digital Charter*
  - Canada's Digital Charter emphasizes the importance of digital literacy and control over personal data. While it doesn't specifically mandate digital well-being practices, its principles support a framework for responsible digital engagement.
- *Belgium's Work Email Limits*
  - Following France's lead, Belgium introduced measures for public sector employees that limit sending work-related emails outside of office hours, highlighting the importance of work-life balance.
- *Japan's "Work Style Reform"*
  - Japan has introduced reforms aimed at reducing the notorious overtime culture. While not solely focused on digital communication, these reforms encourage a better balance between work and private life, indirectly addressing digital burnout.
- *Philippines' Mental Health Act*
  - The Philippines passed a Mental Health Act that, among other provisions, aims to improve the mental health of

workers by tackling stress and promoting work-life balance. This indirectly affects digital well-being by encouraging employers to look at the digital demands placed on employees.

- *Italy's Right to Disconnect*
  - ○ Italy also has introduced the right to disconnect, allowing workers to abstain from digital communication outside work hours without facing disciplinary action.
- *Nordic Work-Life Balance Policies*
  - ○ Nordic countries, known for their high quality of life, have work-life balance policies that extend to digital well-being. Although not always specific to digital usage, these policies create an environment where being constantly online is discouraged after work hours.

These policies demonstrate a growing international acknowledgment of the negative impacts of constant digital connectivity. By legislating and setting guidelines around digital use, these countries are taking proactive steps to safeguard their citizens' mental health and foster environments where digital tools serve to improve life, not detract from it.

Each of these initiatives reflects cultural nuances and approaches to technology, offering a diverse range of strategies from which other nations can draw inspiration. These policies are part of a broader recognition that the digital world must be managed thoughtfully to support citizens' health and well-being in the 21st century.

Corporate Strategies Worldwide: Fostering Employee Digital Well-being

As the digital landscape evolves, companies around the globe are adopting various strategies to ensure the digital well-being of their employees. Here's a glimpse into the corporate world's approaches to nurturing a healthier work-life balance:

- *Flexible Work Arrangements*
  - ○ Companies like Dell and Unilever have embraced flexible work schedules, allowing employees to choose when and where they work. This autonomy enables staff to work during their most productive hours and reduce the strain of constant connectivity.
- *Tech-Free Retreats and Meetings*
  - ○ Some organizations, including Google and LinkedIn, have started conducting regular tech-free retreats or meetings. These allow employees to disconnect, foster face-to-face interaction, and focus on strategic thinking without digital interruptions.
- *Mental Health Days*
  - ○ Recognizing the importance of mental health, firms such as Salesforce and EY offer mental health days. Employees are encouraged to take time off to recharge, with the understanding that this will ultimately improve productivity and creativity.
- *Mindfulness and Wellness Programs*
  - ○ Many companies, including Apple and Aetna, have implemented mindfulness and wellness programs that provide resources such as meditation apps, wellness challenges, or in-house yoga classes to reduce digital stress.
- *Email Etiquette Policies*
  - ○ German auto manufacturer Volkswagen famously implemented an email server blackout period after work hours to prevent employees from receiving work-related emails, encouraging them to disconnect once they leave the office.
- *Education and Training*
  - ○ Firms like Accenture offer workshops and training sessions focused on digital wellness, educating employees about the signs of digital burnout and strategies to cultivate a healthier relationship with technology.

- *Digital Well-being Software*
  - Companies are increasingly using software solutions that monitor usage patterns and prompt breaks or periods of disconnection. For instance, software like Time Doctor or RescueTime helps track and manage employees' digital habits.
- *"No Meeting" Days*
  - Asana and Slack have implemented "no meeting" days where employees are not required to attend any meetings, freeing up time for focused, uninterrupted work or downtime away from screens.
- *Remote Work Support*
  - Organizations have started to provide more support for remote workers to establish clear boundaries between work and personal life. This includes stipends for home office setups, digital wellness resources, or guidelines for communication.
- *Health-Oriented Office Design*
  - Some companies are reimagining office spaces to promote health. For example, Amazon's Seattle headquarters features spaces that resemble greenhouses, filled with plants to create a calming environment that encourages breaks from screens.

The strategies companies employ are as diverse as their corporate cultures, but they all share a common goal: to create a sustainable and healthy working environment that acknowledges the importance of digital well-being. These initiatives reflect an understanding that employee well-being directly impacts productivity, engagement, and overall company success. As we move further into the digital age, corporate strategies for digital well-being will likely become a standard, integral part of organizational health and culture.

11

Epilogue

Personal Reflection on Digital Balance

As we draw the curtains on this exploration of analog anchoring in a digitized world, I find myself in a quiet moment of introspection, reflecting on my own journey towards digital balance.

The quest for equilibrium in the digital age is as personal as it is universal. My own story is a tapestry woven with threads of struggle against the allure of ceaseless connectivity and an earnest desire for presence in the palpable world around me. It has been a journey marked by moments of profound connection with people and nature, punctuated by lapses into the seductive embrace of digital consumption.

Acknowledging the Challenge: In admitting the power technology holds over my daily life, I found the first seeds of resistance. The acknowledgment that my attention, once scattered across the endless digital expanse, could be reclaimed and refocused on the here and now was a revelation. This book was born from that very revelation — the realization that technology, when used mindfully, could become a tool for enhancement rather than a leash.

Embracing Analog Moments: The tactile joy of turning the pages of a beloved book, the earthy scent of garden soil between my fingers, the warmth of shared laughter with friends — these experiences are the

144

anchors of my existence. They offer a counterbalance to the weight of a hyperconnected life, providing refuge and grounding.

The Path of Mindfulness: Mindfulness has been a compass on this voyage. It has taught me to observe my interactions with technology, to pause before reaching for my phone, and to ask, "Is this serving me, or am I serving it?" This mindful approach has not been about renunciation but about harmonizing my digital and analog lives.

Respecting Individuality: Every person's balance point is unique. My balance involves hours spent in writing, occasionally interrupted by the necessity of digital communication, while for others, it might be entirely different. Respecting our individual needs and boundaries is crucial in this balancing act.

Future Aspirations: As I look ahead, my aspiration is to continue nurturing this balance, to live deliberately with technology as my ally, not my master. I hope to embrace innovation while advocating for spaces that respect our need for presence. I envision a future where technology supports our well-being and enriches our lives without diminishing the quality of our human experiences.

A Call to Community: I extend an invitation to you, the reader, to join me in this continual balancing act. Let us create communities that foster both technological advancement and the richness of analog life. Let us teach the next generation the value of presence, the beauty of the tangible world, and the power of human connection.

Gratitude and Hope: I conclude with gratitude for the digital tools that have enabled me to share these thoughts and for the analog spaces that have given them depth and color. In this balance, I find hope — hope for a future where we wield technology with intention and wisdom, crafting a world that cherishes the physical touch as much as the digital click.

As you close this book and return to the world, a world ever oscillating between the analog and the digital, may you find your balance, your joy, and your anchoring.

This reflective epilogue serves not only as a personal testament to the author's journey but also as an open letter to readers, inviting them to consider their own relationships with technology and the physical world. It aims to inspire, guide, and offer solace in the shared challenges we face in finding our individual and collective equilibriums.

12

Resources and Further Reading

In providing a resource list for further reading, it's essential to offer a curated selection that spans a range of perspectives and insights into the intersection of technology, society, and the personal quest for balance. Below is an example of how such a list might be structured, including books, articles, and other materials that could be beneficial for readers seeking to delve deeper into these topics.

Resources and Further Reading

i. Books:

- "Digital Minimalism: Choosing a Focused Life in a Noisy World" by Cal Newport
    - Explores the philosophy of digital minimalism, which helps to declutter and focus digital life.
- "The Shallows: What the Internet Is Doing to Our Brains" by Nicholas Carr

- An in-depth look at how the internet is changing our cognitive processes.
- "Reclaiming Conversation: The Power of Talk in a Digital Age" by Sherry Turkle
  - Discusses the importance of face-to-face conversation and its struggle to survive against digital communication.
- "Technopoly: The Surrender of Culture to Technology" by Neil Postman
  - Examines the impact of technology on society and culture.
- "Irresistible: The Rise of Addictive Technology and the Business of Keeping Us Hooked" by Adam Alter
  - An analysis of why we can't stop scrolling, swiping, clicking and watching.

ii. Articles and Journals:

- "Mindful Tech: Bringing Balance to Our Digital Lives" by David M. Levy
  - An exploration of how we can use technology in a way that is reflective, intentional, and mindful.
- "The Attention Merchants: The Epic Scramble to Get Inside Our Heads" by Tim Wu
  - Looks at how our attention is captured and commodified by technology.
- "Can We Be Alone Together?" by Sherry Turkle (published in Psychology Today)
  - A short article on the paradox of being 'alone together' in the digital age.
- "A Manifesto for Slow Communication" by John Freeman (published in The Wall Street Journal)
  - Argues for a more measured and reflective mode of communication.

iii. Documentaries and Videos:

- "The Social Dilemma" (Netflix)
  - A documentary-drama hybrid that explores the dangerous human impact of social networking.
- "Screened Out" (Available on multiple streaming platforms)
  - A documentary focusing on our obsession with screen time.

iv. Websites and Online Resources:

- Center for Humane Technology (humane tech.com)
  - An organization leading the charge on realigning technology with humanity's best interests.
- Mindful Schools (mindfulschools.org)
  - Resources for educators and parents to integrate mindfulness practices into education.
- Digital Wellness Institute (digitalwellnessinstitute.com)
  - Offers courses and certifications on digital wellness.

v. Podcasts:

- "Note to Self"
  - Explores how we can maintain humanity in the digital age.
- "Time Well Spent"
  - Discusses technology, attention, and the fight for a better future.

vi. Communities and Forums:

- Reddit communities like r/digitalminimalism and r/nosurf
  - Forums for sharing experiences and tips for minimizing digital distractions.
- Meetup groups focused on digital wellness and mindfulness

○ Local and virtual meetups can provide community support for those seeking balance.

This collection of resources offers a range of entry points for readers of varying familiarity with the subject matter. It's designed to inspire continued learning and self-exploration, encouraging readers to seek out information and communities that resonate with their personal journey towards finding balance in a digitized world.

About The Author

David Olubiyi is a thought leader and pioneer in the realm of digital wellness and mindfulness. With a unique background in physics, he brings a scientific perspective to his exploration of the intersection between technology and human well-being.

In his book, "Analog Anchors: Grounding Yourself in the Digital Tide," David draws upon his extensive experience to guide readers through the challenges of the digital era. His passion for promoting a balanced lifestyle in an increasingly connected world is evident in his innovative concepts and practical strategies for digital detoxification and analog engagement.

David holds a master's degree from the University of Lethbridge and has been a prominent keynote speaker at various events focusing on digital health and mindfulness. His work encompasses scholarly research as well as hands-on workshops and seminars, where he empowers individuals to reclaim their attention and foster a deeper connection with the analog world.

Through his writing, speaking, and teaching, David seeks to inspire a movement towards intentional living. His philosophy is centered on using technology as a tool for enhancement rather than a source of constant distraction. He advocates not for the rejection of the digital world, but for finding harmony and establishing a mindful relationship with technology.

"Analog Anchors: Grounding Yourself in the Digital Tide" represents the culmination of David Olubiyi's years of exploration and expertise. This book offers a beacon of hope and practical advice for those seeking to navigate the digital tide with grace and purpose, making it a must-read for anyone looking to balance their digital and analog lives.